The Macat Library

世界思想宝库钥匙丛书

解析阿尔君·阿帕杜莱

《消失的现代性：全球化的文化维度》

AN ANALYSIS OF

ARJUN APPADURAI'S

MODERNITY AT LARGE

Cultural Dimensions of Globalization

Amy Young Evrard ◎ 著

李磊 ◎ 译

上海外语教育出版社
外教社 SHANGHAI FOREIGN LANGUAGE EDUCATION PRESS

目　录

CONTENTS

引 言

要 点

- 阿尔君·阿帕杜莱 1949 年出生于印度孟买。1967 年他来到美国，在美国学习、工作至今。由于拥有在印度和美国两个国家生活的经历，他对文化和全球化*（对全球范围内互联互通的世界所产生的文化、社会效应进行的研究）形成了自己独到的见解。

- 阿帕杜莱在《消失的现代性》一书中另辟蹊径。此前，对于全球化的认识和描述往往集中在经济或政治领域，阿帕杜莱关注的却是全球化中的人、文化、思想。

- 对于有志于了解、研究全球化的人类学家*和地理学家*来说，《消失的现代性》是一部有着重要意义的关键性著作。（人类学家致力于对世界上不同民族的信仰、行为进行系统的研究；地理学家研究的是世界的自然特征以及这些自然特征与人口分布、资源分布等因素之间的关系。）

阿尔君·阿帕杜莱其人

《消失的现代性：全球化的文化维度》（1996）一书的作者阿尔君·阿帕杜莱 1949 年出生于印度孟买，并在那里长大。他曾在自己的作品中谈起过自己的童年，表示在童年时代他的"主体性"——他用这个词表示通过文化塑造的自我意识——是"后殖民"的。1858 年至 1947 年间，印度是英国的殖民地（也就是说，那段时间里，印度受到英国的统治和剥削）。阿帕杜莱小时候，英国文化还影响并控制着印度。这种英国文化的影响塑造了他成长阶段的主体性，而美国的文化影响塑造了他成年后的主体性。

1967 年，阿帕杜莱离开印度来到美国，并于 1976 年在芝加哥大学获得哲学博士学位。他当时的研究焦点是现代化——20 世纪中叶西方社会在技术、经济、政治以及各方面的全面进步。

18 岁以后，阿帕杜莱经常在印度和美国之间往返。在他的作品中，他创建了人和思想理念跨越国界和地域进行移动的理论。他指出，不同的人对现代性 *——现代化期间和之后的阶段——的体验由他们的视角决定。对于住在印度和住在美国的不同的人来说，世界看上去可能是不一样的，但是，这些人都在体验着现代性。

1990 年到 1996 年，阿帕杜莱花了六年时间完成了《消失的现代性》一书。那时候，他在宾夕法尼亚大学跨国 * 文化研究中心担任联合主管。此后，他曾在芝加哥大学工作。现在，他在纽约大学工作。

《消失的现代性》的主要内容

《消失的现代性》创造性地构建了一个研究框架，以全球化与现代性的关系为着手点，研究全球化。在阿帕杜莱看来，西方社会科学理论将现代性看作过去与现在之间的一种突然的断裂。他认为，这一理论存在着如下几个问题：首先，现代化理论 *（20 世纪50 年代和 60 年代在美国社会学 * 领域兴起的研究方法，旨在研究和解释传统社会如何在 20 世纪中叶不断发展，在技术、经济、政治和其他各领域取得与西方社会相应的进步）相信，"西方"是现代的，"其余地区"需要获得西方的帮助才能实现现代性。其次，根据传统的观念，全球化总是导致同质化 *（比如，不同的社会在向西方现代性发展转型的过程中会变得越来越相像）。阿帕杜莱对此持否定意见。在他看来，全球化以及与之相应产生的去国土化 *

（人、物与其原生地的关系变得愈发疏离）意味着现代化并不一定意味着进步性与同质性。

阿帕杜莱相信，他的断裂＊理论可以帮助人们更好地理解全球化的世界。所谓断裂，指的是人和观念脱离其原生地的趋势。阿帕杜莱希望后来的学者能够紧跟他的步伐，研究世界范围内各种新型的"全球文化流动"＊。其中，迁移＊（人从一个地方到另一个地方的移动）与电子媒体＊（使图像和观点不断增殖、传播的技术）是最重要的两种流动。阿帕杜莱认为它们是文化变革的核心力量，特别是在其《消失的现代性》一书出版前的二十年里。这些流动使世界上充满了不同的身份。

人与图像的流动带来了"想象的工作"。在阿帕杜莱看来，想象"在许多社会中已成为普通人群日常精神活动的一部分"。[1] 人们在世界上不同的国家和地区间移动，接受大众传媒带来的各类信息，具备了想象新的人生和新的世界的能力。这是现代主体性的重要部分：人们通过把自己想象为现代的，利用想象的力量将现代性转化为现实。

现代的社会想象＊（一种有组织的社会实践，通过这种社会想象，个人与社会群体构想了理想的生活形式，并努力实现这种新的可能性）打破了曾经被认为是现代性标志的体制、机制。现在，很多人都生活在流离＊中，原生于特定地点的社会群体现在四散在世界各地。但是，不论他们现在生活在哪个单一民族国家里，流离的群体还是会继续想象他们自己的故国家园。这一部分是由于他们都接受了大众媒体形象，这些形象增强了他们自己的流离身份认同。这就是世界正如何变得"后民族"＊的一个例子。

在《消失的现代性》中，阿帕杜莱号召人类学家发展出新的理论和方法，研究处在流动状态的世界。这些新的理论和方法，应该聚焦全球文化流动的运作方式，并充分考虑社会想象是如何创造了新形式的主体性。

《消失的现代性》使得阿尔君·阿帕杜莱成为全球化研究领域中的重要人类学家。自出版以来，该书对人类学领域的影响历久弥新，已成为该领域中的经典佳作。在谷歌学术上对本书的引用将近两万次。

《消失的现代性》的学术价值

阿帕杜莱 1996 年出版了《消失的现代性》。那时候，人类学家习惯于将研究聚焦于定居在一个地方的小型社会群体，正苦于如何寻找到新的研究方法来对全球化的世界进行反思与研究。阿帕杜莱认为，人类学的研究方法应该认识到，现在世界各地在全球化浪潮中都是互相联系着的了。他建议人类学研究者对迁移和电子媒体等全球流动进行研究。

阿帕杜莱的书让此前惯于把研究对象当作固定不变事物的人类学家将研究转向了流动的文化。书中提出流动文化的研究可以借用文化研究领域的模型范式。许多人类学家接受了阿帕杜莱提出的挑战，拓展了对于文化的理解，将全球化的影响纳入其中。

研究全球化的人类学家努力在两种不同方法中寻得一种平衡。一种方法强调全球化如何通过文化帝国主义 *（强大社会的文化压倒或取代了弱小社会的文化的过程）使世界变得更加同质化。另一种方法强调的却正好相反：全球化如何让世界变得更加多元化。比方说，迁移与媒体就不断创造出新的或者混合的文化形式。阿帕杜莱更支持第二种方法。

还有一些人类学家认为，造成贫困、绝望、移位是全球化最重要的一个方面。尽管阿帕杜莱也反思了全球化的弊端，但是在《消失的现代性》一书的结尾，他还是表示出了乐观的态度。全球文化流动使草根社会运动变成可能，与全球化造成的严酷后果进行抗衡。（草根社会运动指的是自下而上，由社会成员而非社会领导人组织的社会运动。）

　　对于将全球化研究聚焦于经济和政治领域的人来说，这本书可能没有那么有说服力。

---

1. 阿尔君·阿帕杜莱：《消失的现代性：全球化的文化维度》，明尼阿波利斯：明尼苏达大学出版社，1996年，第5页。

第一部分：学术渊源

1 作者生平与历史背景

要点 🔑

- 《消失的现代性》是有关全球化*的关键性的人类学*著作，在谷歌学术上被引用次数将近两万次。

- 阿尔君·阿帕杜莱在印度出生和长大，成年后来到了美国。这样的经历对他的理论产生了深远的影响，他相信，人和观念都不再局限于固定的地区或区域。

- 阿帕杜莱的《消失的现代性》一书受众广泛，涵盖了人类学、区域研究*（对某一特定地理地区或民族地区进行的跨学科研究）、全球化等领域。这本书中独创的许多重要术语现在仍被人类学家广泛使用。

为何要读这部著作？

阿尔君·阿帕杜莱现任纽约大学媒体、文化与传播学院戈达德讲席教授。1996 年，他出版了《消失的现代性：全球化的文化维度》一书，他指出，在全球文化流动*（全球化带来的全球文化维度或领域的活动）理念的基础上，应建立起一套新的理论框架或者工作方法。全球文化流动理念能够帮助我们更好地研究现代化、全球化世界中的文化。

阿帕杜莱认为，此前学界对文化的研究和分析都局限于某一个特定的地区，这种方法已经无法适用于现在的新形势。在阿帕杜莱提出的新研究框架中，学者们能够更好地研究理念、事物、人如何通过全球文化流动在世界各地活动。其中，全球文化流动包括了迁移*（人离开出生国来到不同的国家生活）和电子媒体*（互联网、电视、电影等）。

迁移和电子媒体影响了社会想象*——人们对他们的生活和他们的世界进行集体想象的方法。这为人们确立自我身份带来了许多新的可能性。

此前，人类学家苦苦寻求更好的方法和理论以期更好地理解全球化时代中的文化。阿帕杜莱独到的见解无疑为他们指明了新的方向。此外，这本书也鼓励人们在研究全球化的过程中充分认识并重视文化这一重要核心元素。

> "大规模迁移的故事（无论是主动的还是被动的）在人类历史上并不是什么新鲜事。但是，当大规模迁移和经由大众媒介传播的图像、文本、感觉叠加在一起，就在现代主体性的确立过程中形成了一种新的不稳定秩序。"
>
> —— 阿尔君·阿帕杜莱：《消失的现代性：全球化的文化维度》

作者生平

阿帕杜莱 1949 年出生于印度孟买，并在那里长大。在童年时代，他的主体性*，或者说他的自我意识深受周围的文化影响：英国对印度的殖民统治残留余波，美国的媒体和流行文化盛极一时。1967 年，阿帕杜莱离开印度来到美国读书并定居。他的妻子是美国印度历史专家卡罗尔·布雷肯里奇*。阿帕杜莱经常在印度和美国两国之间往返，受个人经历的影响，他对人与观念的全球流动有着深入的见解。

阿帕杜莱 1976 年在芝加哥大学获得哲学博士学位，此后在耶鲁大学、宾夕法尼亚大学、芝加哥大学、普林斯顿大学、纽约大学等美国著名高校执教。

阿帕杜莱用他个人的经历阐发自己的理念。他在书中写到，有一次，他和妻子及 11 岁大的儿子回到印度，他的儿子在那里见到了许多在个人生活或职业生涯中与印度、美国或其他国家有千丝万缕联系的家人，遇到了"许多变动的传记所组成的网络"[1]——与传统、家庭、个人身份建立关系的不同方法。

在阿帕杜莱看来，构建个人身份的是多种不同线索，我们应该集中精力书写一种新的民族志*。民族志指的是文化人类学家采取的一种调研方法或由此形成的研究成果。一般来说，民族志的写作需要长期在一个地区生活，观察并参与当地人的生活。阿帕杜莱认为，民族志的研究应该"将想象从地域的限制中解放出来"[2]。人们在世界各地移动，在不同的地方工作和生活，他们想象和经历自己的生活的方式已经发生了巨大的变化。从某种程度上说，他们不会再简单地通过自己的出生地来定义自己，而是会通过他们遇到的人和理念形成自我身份认同。

创作背景

阿帕杜莱成长于 20 世纪五六十年代的印度。当时，印度实现了独立，在建立国家和民族身份的过程中正经历着后殖民*困境。尽管英国的殖民于 1947 年就已经结束了，但是，在阿帕杜莱小时候，印度却依然深受英国文化的影响。不过，很快情况就发生了变化，因为印度确立了自己作为新兴后殖民国家的身份。

对统一的印度身份的寻求很快就被印度国内种族、宗教身份的多样性分裂*了。其中，印度的一些种族、宗教群体甚至跨过了国界，进入了其他国家。殖民的结束带来了民族自决的新的可能性。因此，在后殖民时期，南亚地理上的国界线不断发生着变化，整个南亚地区充斥着不同族群和国家间争夺政治权力及其他权力的斗争和冲突。

阿帕杜莱 1967 年来到美国后，他学习了人类学、区域研究以及 "无往不胜的现代化理论*形式——在当时两极对立的世界里，这是美国精神的可靠保障"[3]。现代化理论由美国的社会学家*（研究社会特点、形成和历史的学者）于 20 世纪五六十年代提出，旨在研究和解释传统社会如何不断发展，在技术、经济、政治和其他各领域取得与西方社会那样的进步。那时候，美国正处在冷战中，与苏联及其盟国在政治和军事方面剑拔弩张。当时，学者和普通美国民众都认为美国是现代性*的最佳例证，与之相对的是他们认为落后、压抑的苏联。

阿帕杜莱在印度和美国两个国家成长生活的经历塑造了他的学术生涯。《消失的现代性》一书是他对美国社会科学界关于现代性和现代化的理论的反思。比方说，美国社会科学界普遍认为，西方社会取得的发展和进步带来了现代性，而现代性是具有普世价值的，是全世界人民共同向往的。但是，在这本书中，阿帕杜莱却引用了发生在后殖民时期的印度的例子来讨论身份认同和种族暴力问题。从这本书我们可以看出，阿帕杜莱的研究和生活都受到了来自不同社会的理念和印象的影响。

1. 阿尔君·阿帕杜莱:《消失的现代性:全球化的文化维度》,明尼阿波利斯:明尼苏达大学出版社,1996 年,第 57 页。
2. 阿帕杜莱:《消失的现代性》,第 58 页。
3. 阿帕杜莱:《消失的现代性》,第 2 页。

2 学术背景

要点 ⚷⊶┤

- 文化人类学*研究的是人类生存的文化层面。

- 虽然阿帕杜莱是一位文化人类学家,《消失的现代性》一书依托的却主要是其他学科的理论,其中包括政治学家、历史学家本尼迪克特·安德森*提出的用"想象的力量构建共同体"的理论。

- 阿帕杜莱认为,人类学家可以学习借鉴文化研究*的方法。

著作语境

阿尔君·阿帕杜莱在写作《消失的现代性:全球化的文化维度》一书时(1990—1996)对美国人类学家广泛使用的方法提出了挑战。德裔美国人类学家弗朗兹·博厄斯*是公认的美国人类学之父。他对人类文化的普遍性理论嗤之以鼻,推崇对某一特定地点进行长期的民族志*研究,收集具有描述性的实证*数据(也就是说,通过长期观察和采访收集可证实的信息)。

与博厄斯等美国人类学家不同的是,阿帕杜莱提倡的是对全球和地区都进行民族志研究。在这方面,他受到了其他人类学家的影响。比方说,在 20 世纪 70 年代和 80 年代里,人类学家研究了不同的社会如何通过贸易和其他国际流动联系在一起。

《消失的现代性》认为,过去很长一段时间以来,全球不同的社会通过贸易和其他方式彼此互动交流。然而,在 20 世纪 80 年代和 90 年代中,随着交通和通讯成本大幅降低,这种国际间的交流得以大大增进。不论是人还是理念,都可以在世界各地快速移动,这样，人和理念就不再局限于某一特定地区。阿帕杜莱指出，人类学必须发展出新的理论和方法来研究全球文化流动＊以及这种流动对特定的地点产生了怎样的影响。

> "真正世界主义的民族志实践，需要对当今美国的文化研究领域做出诠释，也需要阐释此领域内人类学的现状。"
>
> —— 阿尔君·阿帕杜莱：《消失的现代性：全球化的文化维度》

学科概览

虽然阿帕杜莱写作时以人类学家为自己的目标受众，他的作品却主要受到了人类学之外的领域的影响。比方说，他受到了旨在对金钱、资源、权力在全球范围内的分布方式和原因进行描述的世界体系理论＊的影响。世界体系理论家主要包括社会学家伊曼纽尔·沃勒斯坦＊，他提出"中心"＊（发达）国家和"边缘"＊（发展中）国家之间存在一种关系结构，以此来分析全球范围内政治和经济方面的不平等。

阿帕杜莱等人类学家也受到了德国政治哲学家、经济学家卡尔·马克思＊的影响。马克思认为，经济体制内蕴含着的矛盾冲突是带来历史性改变的主要力量，我们对文化进行的研究不可能与社会结构和权力关系割裂开来。

此外，阿帕杜莱认为，全球文化流动的散裂＊与社会想象＊的工作也使全球范围内的不公情况和权力分布情况变得愈发复杂。（当两种不同的流动造成了互相矛盾、彼此冲突的情况时，即产生了散裂。）阿帕杜莱写道："即使最凄惨最无望的生活、最残酷最无人性的处境、最严酷的活生生的不平等，现在都对想象的作用开放了。"[1] 换句话说，即使全球化*给人们带来了不幸，人们还是具备能动性*（在特定情况下做出选择和行动的能力），他们可以选择自己想象新世界、新生活的方式。

政治学家、历史学家本尼迪克特·安德森对想象在政治上的作用有所研究。安德森认为，报纸和书籍——"印刷资本主义"*——的生产和流通，促进了民族主义*（一种意识形态，坚信对族群或民族国家的认同或兴趣的重要性）情绪的产生，从而造就了"想象的共同体"*（一群从未遇见过彼此的人仍坚信彼此身份中的很重要的一部分是相同的）。

阿帕杜莱认为，对于安德森所描述的这个过程，全球化正在起着加速及强化作用。现在，想象的共同体能够跨越民族或区域的边界。

学术渊源

许多不同学科的学者都认识到权力和统治在理解文化的过程中的重要性。因此，他们发展出一种"文化帝国主义*导致全球范围内文化同质化*"的理论：各具特色的本土文化最终都将不复存在，全球范围内，不同民族在文化方面将变得愈发相似。对此，阿帕杜莱持反对意见。他相信，全球化将带来文化的异质化*，在全球化的影响下，必将出现新的、多元混杂的文化形式。

阿帕杜莱在写作《消失的现代性》期间，深入地参与到关于全球化和跨国主义（一种强调全球联系的理论视角）的讨论中来。他在普林斯顿高等研究院担任麦克阿瑟学者*时萌生出了写作这本书的想法和思路，并于担任宾夕法尼亚大学跨国*文化研究中心联合主任期间开始了这本书的写作。最终，在芝加哥大学创办全球化项目（一群来自不同学科的学者共同研究国家间在经济、政治和文化方面的联系）并担任负责人期间，他完成了这本书的写作。

在人类学研究领域，阿帕杜莱以注重研究文化的全球维度而著称。他的一大突出贡献就是架起了人类学与其他全球化研究领域的桥梁。

---

1. 阿尔君·阿帕杜莱：《消失的现代性：全球化的文化维度》，明尼阿波利斯：明尼苏达大学出版社，1996年，第54页。

3 主导命题

要点 🔑

- 阿帕杜莱认为，研究全球化 * 的文化维度，应研究全球文化流动 *。他指出，迁移 * 和电子媒体 * 使人与理念在全球范围内广泛流动，具有重要研究价值。

- 在《消失的现代性》出版前，研究全球化的学者们主要关注的是全球范围内存在的不平等问题及其如何导致了文化同质化 *——世界上不同社会的文化面貌正变得愈发相似。或者他们根本就没有注意到全球化的文化维度。

- 在阿帕杜莱看来，全球化带来了文化的异质化 *——世界上不同社会的文化正变得愈发多元。为此，他需要找到新的理论和方法来研究当今世界。

核心问题

20 世纪 90 年代，阿尔君·阿帕杜莱开始创作《消失的现代性：全球化的文化维度》一书时，他正在参与全球化问题的研究。研究全球化的理论家们往往更关注全球化的政治和经济维度，但是，阿帕杜莱却认为全球化的文化维度有着重要的研究价值。

阿帕杜莱的主要研究领域是人类学 *。在这一领域，已经有学者开始关注全球化对本土文化的影响。此前，美国的人类学家更多的是透过整体论的视角对小规模的、相对独立的社会进行研究。所谓整体论，是一种强调文化信仰和行为如何作为一个整体的系统进行运作的文化研究视角。

阿帕杜莱和其他人类学家对此持否定意见。他们认识到，即使是看上去相对独立的地区其实也受到了全球文化流动的影响，因此，他们赞成使用新的方法和理论。阿帕杜莱等人类学家强调的是断裂*——文化实践活动从其原生地脱离、断裂开来，而非整体论。

越来越多的人离开自己的出生国，在其他地方生活，在许多地方旅行，吸收不同地区文化的影响。现代人类学应当反映出这种以全新的方式愈演愈烈的国际间的文化流动并采取新的研究方式。

> "当下国际交流的核心问题是文化同质化与文化异质化之间的矛盾。"
>
> —— 阿尔君·阿帕杜莱:《消失的现代性：全球化的文化维度》

参与者

阿帕杜莱与其他研究全球化的学者保持着沟通与交流，一起寻找着关于异质化与同质化、权力、不公等问题的答案。他们希望创立新的理论和方法，以理解和把握去国土化*进程与全球文化流动。

在人类学领域之外，学者们也关注着全球化可能带来的同质化问题，特别是文化帝国主义*在这个过程中的作用。例如，英国诺丁汉特伦特大学研究英语、文化、传媒的约翰·汤姆林森*教授就把全球化描述为"在世界范围内建立起基本社会文化现实的西方版本的过程：西方的……理论、价值观、伦理体系、理性主义的方法、强调科技的世界观、政治文化等"。[1]西方通过文化帝国主义统治世界，不仅传播西方的食物、潮流、语言，更传播西方的世界观和价值观。

人类学家整体上来说同意阿帕杜莱关于文化异质化的论点，批评汤姆林森等学者过于简单地把非西方国家看作西方产品和理念的被动接受者。其中最重要的人类学家就是瑞典斯德哥尔摩大学的荣休教授乌尔夫·翰纳兹*。对于阿帕杜莱提出的关于不同种族在世界范围内进行跨国交往的理论，翰纳兹表示赞同，并提出了"全球家园"*2一词。所谓全球家园，指的是不同的社会、经济体、文化构成了一个互联互通的世界。

此外，翰纳兹在阿帕杜莱基础上更进一步，指出受到全球化影响的人依旧能够获得能动性*，即自由的选择。他描述了生活在非西方社会的人们如何通过他所说的克里奥尔化*（多种文化形式的混合）对全球化作出自己的回应。3

当时的论战

阿帕杜莱认为，正是因为有了文化的异质化，我们的时代才具有了现代性*。在全球范围内，人与理念广泛流动，不论是个人还是群体，都可以想象新的身份和新的生活。他们可以在交汇融合的文化形式、实践和理念中建构起他们想象中的生活。对此，阿帕杜莱举了板球运动等例子。殖民*时期（英国对印度统治和剥削的高峰期），英国人将板球运动带到了印度。19 世纪末，印度上层人士开始玩板球。那时候，板球运动体现的是英国上层人士的男性魅力。现在，前英国殖民地和其他世界各国的人都在玩板球，板球运动员来自不同的种族，有不同的宗教信仰；板球运动受到了媒体的广泛关注和报道。板球运动的流行是文化异质化的绝佳案例。只有从历史角度进行深入挖掘，我们才能真正地理解这项运动。

现在，关于文化与全球化的讨论还在继续。包括翰纳兹在内的学者们创作出了许多关于迁移、媒体和其他文化流动的学术著作。但是，在研究全球化的文化维度方面，阿帕杜莱以其提出的新概念、创造的新词语（"族群景观"等术语）以及令人心悦诚服的写作风格无疑将继续指引着我们前进。

---

1. 约翰·汤姆林森："国际主义，全球化及文化帝国主义"，《媒介与文化规则》，肯尼思·汤普森编，伦敦：赛奇出版社，1998 年，第 14 页。
2. 乌尔夫·翰纳兹：《文化复杂性：社会组织意义研究》，纽约：哥伦比亚大学出版社，1992 年，第 217 页。
3. 翰纳兹：《文化复杂性》，第 256 页。

4 作者贡献

要点 🔑

- 阿帕杜莱写作《消失的现代性》的主要目标是促进新理论、新方法的产生，以期通过全球文化流动这一理论框架更好地理解全球化。

- 阿帕杜莱主要关注的是迁移 * 和电子媒体 * 如何促进了新形式的社会想象 * 的产生。

- 该书在之前现代性 * 和想象理论的基础上展现了现代世界的主要特征，即全世界范围内人与理念的新的、更深刻的互动交流。

作者目标

纵观《消失的现代性：全球化的文化维度》一书，阿尔君·阿帕杜莱的目标是说明在去国土化 *（人与物与其原生地的联系愈发疏离）的世界里，迁移和媒体如何通过社会想象的作用对社会产生影响。在这本书问世之前，对全球化的研究主要集中在经济和政治领域，认为经济和政治才是全球化过程和结构的主要形成因素，人和理念的全球流通只不过是全球化的产物，而不是成因。

阿帕杜莱关注两种全球文化流动：迁移和电子媒体。他认为，迁移和电子媒体是全球化的重要组成部分，是带来改变的巨大力量。因为有了迁移和电子媒体，人们可以一起想象新的生活和新的世界，在此前的历史阶段里，这种社会想象是根本不可能实现的。在现代化之前的阶段里，想象被局限在个人和群体的社群或地区中。现在，因为可以接触到来自世界各地的不同的人和不同的理念，人们可以看到并想象自己也拥有不同的思维方式和不同的生活。

> "几个世纪以来，世界一直是大规模沟通交流的聚集体（混杂的集合体）。然而，当今世界面临的是新的、更大强度的沟通交流。"
>
> —— 阿尔君·阿帕杜莱：《消失的现代性：全球化的文化维度》

研究方法

《消失的现代性》激励人类学家和其他学者想象新的理论和方法来理解文化。尽管阿帕杜莱汲取了人类学和区域研究＊等学科之前的理论，但是，对于他们提出的文化与特定地点紧密联系的理论，阿帕杜莱却予以批判。他认为，这个观点即便以前有效，也已无法适应当今世界的实际情况。

阿帕杜莱通过自己独具一格的写作风格再现了全球化的速度、强度和混乱状态。他把宏大的观点和概念一个个抛向读者，飞快地提出一个又一个复杂的例子来解释自己的观点。通过这种方式，他对迁移和电子媒体这两大最重要的全球文化流动进行了解读。

阿帕杜莱认为，迁移和电子媒体，再加上单一民族国家＊的衰落，导致了新的流离＊群体（跨越国界或其他地理界限而存在的群体身份）的产生。在本书的第三部分，阿帕杜莱指出，这些流动对基于共同民族身份而形成的现代运动（阿帕杜莱称其为"文化主义"）起着至关重要的作用。在迁移和电子媒体的作用下，文化主义往往会导致文化或民族冲突。阿帕杜莱关于社会想象的概念展示了全球文化流动如何既创造群体身份，又带来群体间的冲突和矛盾。

时代贡献

西方社会科学理论往往认定现代性是种普遍向往的状态，对此，阿帕杜莱持反对意见。这个论调出现于现代化理论*中。现代化理论是 20 世纪 50 年代和 60 年代在美国社会学领域兴起的理论流派，受到了德国社会学家马克思·韦伯*和法兰克福学派*（在德国法兰克福大学社会研究中心兴起的社会思想学派，受到了德国政治哲学家卡尔·马克思的影响，对资本主义进行了批判）的影响。现代化理论相信，"想象将被资本主义、世俗化和其他促进全球化的过程阻碍"[1]。

但是，公众的想象并不会被阻碍。"遍布全球的对大众媒体的消费往往会激发抗拒、反讽、选择，或者一言以蔽之，它激发了能动性。"[2] 个体和社群并不仅仅被动地消费电子媒体带来的信息，他们会利用电子媒体构建自己的身份。

为了证明这一点，阿帕杜莱对政治学家、历史学家本尼迪克特·安德森*提出的"想象的共同体"*理念进行了进一步的挖掘与发挥。安德森认为，印刷资本主义*（书籍杂志等民族媒体）的发展使不同群体的人们发展出了一种共同的身份。通过阅读用同一种语言写就的报纸杂志和书籍等，单一民族国家的公民形成了一种民族主义的感觉。在此基础上，阿帕杜莱提出了"情感共同体"的概念，"这一群体能够共同想象和感受事物"[3]。这种通过迁移和大众媒体产生的集体想象，使人们建立起了一种超越民族和其他地域界限的共同的身份。

阿帕杜莱的观点极具独创性，因为他关注的是"能使想象的作用得以转变的日常文化实践"[4]。他希望能够建立起一种理论方法，以真实地反映出人们并不仅仅是简单地接受和遵从社会环境中的规则和标准，人们还会集体协作，想象出新的规则和标准。

1. 阿尔君·阿帕杜莱：《消失的现代性：全球化的文化维度》，明尼阿波利斯：明尼苏达大学出版社，1996年，第6页。
2. 阿帕杜莱：《消失的现代性》，第7页。
3. 阿帕杜莱：《消失的现代性》，第8页。
4. 阿帕杜莱：《消失的现代性》，第9页。

第二部分：学术思想

5 思想主脉

要点 ⚷━

- 阿帕杜莱在《消失的现代性》一书中强调了三个关键性问题：描述了全球文化流动*的五个维度；探索了迁移*和电子媒体*在人们想象自己、想象世界的过程中产生的影响；介绍了一个研究文化和全球化*的新框架。

- 他的主要论点是，对全球化的分析研究核心应该是文化，而不是经济。

- 阿帕杜莱的论点涵盖范围广泛且全面。他从殖民*时期的印度和当代印度找了一些例子支撑自己的论点。

核心主题

在《消失的现代性：全球化的文化维度》中，阿尔君·阿帕杜莱描述了五种全球文化流动，并将它们称为"景观"*，例如媒体景观、金融景观。全球文化流动是全球化的产物，对个人和社会都有深刻的影响。不同流动之间关系的隔阂造成了散裂*，也就是断裂点。阿帕杜莱敦促我们在全球化的视域里进行研究。

阿帕杜莱最感兴趣的是两种文化流动：通过迁移进行的人的流动，以及通过电子媒体进行的理念的流动。这两种文化流动使人们跨越了原生地或单一民族国家的边界*，面向世界。现在，世界各地的人都可以想象"比以往任何时候都宽广得多的生活的可能性"[1]。

阿帕杜莱对作为名词的"文化"和作为形容词的"文化的"

进行了区分。在 20 世纪大部分时间里，美国人类学家更关注的是本土的和特定的东西，把文化当作"某种对象、物质或实体"[2]进行研究。阿帕杜莱更喜欢的是作为形容词的"文化的"一词，因为它能"将人们带入充满差异、对照和比较的领域，因而更有助益"[3]。文化并不是一个单独的、固定不变的事物，我们从物质的多样性中形成了关于自我和关于世界的概念。阿帕杜莱认为，当代人类学家不能再依赖业已落伍的对身份的认识，而应该更多地关注人如何在现代的全球化的世界中建构身份。人的身份并不仅仅是从出生地或者文化传统中来。人的身份是通过与他们在迁移和电子媒体中接触到的多元的社会进行比较和对比中建构起来的。

"全球生活世界的状况已经发生了整体性的转变。"
—— 阿尔君·阿帕杜莱:《消失的现代性:全球化的文化维度》

思想探究

在书的一开头，阿帕杜莱就回应了现代性*这一问题。所谓现代性，就是 20 世纪与西方国家相关的一套态度、技术和社会形式，现代性也是当下时代的一大特征。阿帕杜莱认为，世界上存在着多种多样的现代性。现在，任何理念在全球范围内流动，差异变得非常明显。因为有差异，人们开始比较，用自己的想象力去理解他们所处的这个特定的地方在全球化的世界里的位置。

《消失的现代性》一书的标题其实就告诉我们，现代性并不存在于某一特定的地点，现代性是"消散"的。在全球化的世界上，生活在不同地方的人可以用不同的方式体验现代性。当不同的文化流动之间出现隔阂或者是矛盾时，在不同的文化流动之间出现隔阂或者是矛盾的地方，差异带来散裂。阿帕杜莱举了一个日本的散裂的例子：日本这个国家对新思想、新观点和外国产品都持有非常开放的态度，但是日本政府却非常不愿意接受外国移民。

为了对散裂进行深入的分析，阿帕杜莱为人类学和其他社会科学提出了一个非常有创新价值的研究框架。在这一框架里，全球文化流动可以被分为五个维度：

- 族群景观 *
- 技术景观 *
- 金融景观 *
- 媒体景观 *
- 意识形态景观 *

以"景观"作为词语的后缀，旨在表现族群、技术、金融、媒体、意识形态在民族国家边界内外的流动性及其形式的不规则性。

族群景观是人的景观，人的身份跨越民族的边界，在民族的边界间移动，甚至对民族的边界产生了影响。阿帕杜莱的族群景观理念强调的是移民、游客以及其他处在活动中的人。技术景观和金融景观指的是技术和金钱的全球模式：它们如何跨越地域的界限发展和流动。媒体景观和意识形态景观都是影像的景观。媒体景观通过电子媒体呈现视觉上的描述，为观者想象自己和想象世界提供素材。意识形态景观往往是与民族或国家的意识形态相关的政治表现和表达。

这个包含五个维度的框架对不同全球文化流动之间的联系与断裂 * 进行了考察与研究。去国土化 * 是这个过程中至关重要的一部分：人、理念、文化形式都离开了原来的背景，进入了新的环境。

语言表述

《消失的现代性》是一本论文集，全书分为三个部分，包含有九篇重新修改过的已发表论文。前三章介绍了本书的主题和主要论点，阐发了阿帕杜莱的"跨国 * 人类学"⁴框架。在这几个章节中，阿帕杜莱表达了对既有的现代性理论的反对意见，并更加重视全球化研究中的文化维度。

本书的目标读者是研究社会科学的学者，特别是研究全球化的学者。书中文字和例子的快速流动生动地再现了全球化背景下人与理念的快速流动。

阿帕杜莱创造了很多新词，比方说"后模糊"（本来已经模糊的边界在全球化影响下变得愈发模糊的状态）、"灰色市场"（正式的也即白色市场与非正式的也即黑色市场之间的经济流动）。他独创的一些新词现在已经成为人类学领域里公认的术语，如"景观""散裂"。在行文的过程里，他假定读者已经掌握了社会科学领域的基本概念，因此，虽然他会对书中每个部分都进行总结，并且在每一个章节的最后都会给出结论，但是因为他的论点实在是涵盖范围太广泛太全面，读者们很难对文章的细节有所把握。

从第四章到第六章，阿帕杜莱通过列举包括消费、时尚、运动、户口调查等英国殖民 * 主义相关的例子，表达了自己的观点。在最后的三章里，阿帕杜莱将视线转向了未来，其中，他特别关注的是后民族 *（作为实体的民族国家不复存在或力量大幅削弱）的世界中民族国家这一模式的未来。

1. 阿尔君·阿帕杜莱:《消失的现代性:全球化的文化维度》,明尼阿波利斯:明尼苏达大学出版社,1996年,第53页。
2. 阿帕杜莱:《消失的现代性》,第12页。
3. 阿帕杜莱:《消失的现代性》,第12页。
4. 阿帕杜莱:《消失的现代性》,第48页。

6 思想支脉

要点 🔑——

- 《消失的现代性》一书中还有一个重要的思想，那就是民族国家处在危机之中，世界正逐渐地呈现出后民族*（在全球化的世界中，民族变得不再那么重要）的特征。

- 文化主义*也多与种族暴力（因种族或民族身份不同而在权力与资源方面分布不均的群体间的暴力行为）联系在一起。

- 尽管种族暴力是本书中的重要话题，阿帕杜莱关于种族暴力的思想却没有得到足够的重视，他最受关注的还是关于现代性*和全球化*的思想。

其他思想

阿尔君·阿帕杜莱在《消失的现代性：全球化的文化维度》一书中还提到了另一个重要思想：民族国家正处在危机之中。在他看来，只有从文化的维度出发才能更好地对民族国家的危机进行理解。人们在身份认同方面已经跨越了民族国家的边界，因此，他们不再对某一个特定的民族身份表示认同。

文化主义与在民族国家层面发生的身份构建息息相关。国家由拥有不同民族身份的人组合而成，但是政府会推行一些观念，告诉人们国家是由某一类特定的人群组成的。这类人群会在群体内部不断努力，以争取获得更多的权益（为某一群体提供利益保障的政府项目），或者在数量上取得优势，以获得安全感。

有些时候，这种行为会变成跨国*行为，因为这些群体会与其他民族国家里与他们有着共同身份认同的群体联系起来，采取行动。比方说，全世界范围内的土著群体会联系在一起，因为他们都有着在各自的民族国家里被边缘化的共同经历。

阿帕杜莱将文化主义与种族暴力问题联系在一起。然而，他在《消失的现代性》一书中对种族暴力的深入探讨并未得到应有的关注，他最出名的还是关于现代性和全球文化流动*的观点。在后来创作的专著中，阿帕杜莱对种族暴力问题进行了进一步的深入挖掘和研究，其中，最出名的一本书是他创作的《少数人的恐惧：关于愤怒地理学》[1]。

> "我相信，民族国家作为一种复杂的现代政治形式正在走向末路。"
>
> —— 阿尔君·阿帕杜莱：《消失的现代性：全球化的文化维度》

思想探究

在阿帕杜莱看来，民族国家"只有作为一个系统的组成部分才有意义"[2]。民族国家的行为已经无法决定历史的进程。其他领域的学者，特别是比较政治学*（对不同国家或不同时代的政治、机构、分歧进行比较的学术研究方法）领域的学者，也认识到了民族国家面临的深重危机。

因为，人们的身份认同已经跨越了民族国家的边界，人们已经不再单纯地把自己的身份和某一个特定的国家联系在一起。在个人与群体的身份建构方面，与民族国家相比，其他的系统和关系（如互相交织的流离*身份、宗教原教旨主义的形式、族群民族主义*）正在发挥着越来越重要的作用。

阿帕杜莱将文化主义理解为"在民族国家层面上调动起来的身份政治"[3]。其中，身份政治指的是以特定的民族、阶级、性别等身份形式为基础的政治观点与政治行为。他从作为名词的"文化"和作为形容词的"文化的"之间的区别入手，对"文化主义"一词进行了界定。在人类学家*看来，文化往往是一种"人类群体拥有的物品或事物"[4]。与之相对应的是作为形容词的"文化的"，它强调的是文化的多维性和多样性，可以让人类学家更多地关注到差异本身[5]。文化并非固定不变，文化更多的是一种身份的维度，只有通过差异与对比才能对其产生更清晰的认识。

文化主义就是为了政治目的（往往是为了对民族国家进行挑战）而利用群体身份。文化主义运动"是想象工作最常见的形式，它经常利用迁移和脱离（地区或群体从一个更大的政治体中独立出来）这一事实或可能性"[6]。阿帕杜莱认为，文化主义是当今世界里文化差异的最重要表现形式，对民族国家来说，文化主义是威胁其稳定的主要因素。

被忽视之处

阿帕杜莱反对将种族身份看作为一种自然的或者是原始的*（一种以共同的生物学本质或亲缘关系带来的强烈情感为基础形成的种族身份界定）状态。在他看来，种族特点是在本土文化与全球文化力量碰撞后建构产生的。

群体的种族身份并不一定是天生的。群体在语言、宗教、食物等文化因素的基础上构建起了种族身份。有时候，这种身份构建发生在更大的范围内，跨过了种族国家的边界。有时候，一个群体会声称他们的身份认同以某一特定地点为基础。

在现代种族国家系统中，种族暴力格外地残酷血腥。阿帕杜莱写道："这些战争中最糟糕的暴力，似乎与日常人际关系和大规模身份认同（由现代民族国家所生产，又被大规模的流离失所而复杂化）之间被扭曲的联系有关。"[7] 阿帕杜莱关于种族暴力的观点可以帮助我们更好地理解其关于全球身份构建的观点与社会想象 * 的作用。社会想象可能会在全球范围内产生作用，使人们具备想象新世界、想象新生活的能力。而种族暴力之所以产生，是因为本土化的身份认同跨越空间上的边界后形成了合力，与民族国家这一概念产生了冲突。

---

1. 阿尔君·阿帕杜莱：《少数人的恐惧：关于愤怒地理学》，北卡罗来纳，杜伦：杜克大学出版社，2006 年。
2. 阿尔君·阿帕杜莱：《消失的现代性：全球化的文化维度》，明尼阿波利斯：明尼苏达大学出版社，1996 年，第 19 页。
3. 阿帕杜莱：《消失的现代性》，第 15 页。
4. 阿帕杜莱：《消失的现代性》，第 12 页。
5. 阿帕杜莱：《消失的现代性》，第 12 页。
6. 阿帕杜莱：《消失的现代性》，第 15 页。
7. 阿帕杜莱：《消失的现代性》，第 154 页。

7 历史成就

要点 🔑

- 阿帕杜莱的《消失的现代性》一书具有划时代的意义，为全球化的背景下进行的文化研究提供了新的视角。

- 该书源于他之前发表的重要学术论文《全球文化经济中的散裂与差异》。在本书中，阿帕杜莱列举了很多案例以论证他的观点：迁移*和电子媒体*对社会想象*产生影响。

- 阿帕杜莱为民族志*研究的发展提出了建议，但是在他自己的研究中，他没有提供任何实证*数据。

观点评价

阿尔君·阿帕杜莱在《消失的现代性：全球化的文化维度》一书中描述了全球文化流动*（特别是迁移和电子媒体）如何帮助人们以新的方式想象世界、想象自己的生活。他展示了这种新的形式在解释当下种族研究和社会活动方面的重要意义。他对自己 1990 年在《理论、文化与社会》[1] 杂志上发表的论文《全球文化经济中的散裂与差异》进行了扩展研究。这篇论文构成了《消失的现代性》一书的第二章。

这篇论文以及这一整本书对学术界最持久、最深远的贡献在于其对"景观"*（包括人、金融、技术、影像与理念的景观）概念的深入研究、详尽阐述。英国的社会学家们，特别是包括马丁·阿尔布劳*等，对"景观"这一理念进行了进一步的拓展，使其进入了其他新领域。阿尔布劳写道："景观这个词为实证的社会研究打开了新的研究视角，使其突破传统的社会和社群理念，更好地对本土／全球之间的关系进行研究。"[2]

> "阿帕杜莱的研究以其社会学想象推动了当下研究的发展。此方面无人能出其右。"
> —— 马丁·阿尔布劳："评《消失的现代性》"，《美国社会学杂志》

当时的成就

阿帕杜莱的论文《全球文化经济中的散裂与差异》是对全球化*的文化维度进行研究的系列论文之一。在这个系列中，来自不同学科领域的学者从各自研究领域出发，研究全球化如何在全球范围内切断了人、文化实践、理念与特定地区的联系。同时，人类学家也在对去国土化*问题进行研究与探讨：去国土化是一种新现象，还是在人类存在所特有的文化交流与改变这同一过程中更快的形式？

全球化研究一直以来都更强调政治和经济因素，认为文化上的变化只不过是全球化影响的一个次要方面，文化因素并不是全球化的重要组成部分。通过《消失的现代性》一书，阿帕杜莱旨在为全球化世界中的文化研究勾勒出一个全新的研究框架。他最大的（同时也是最具争议的）贡献是，他通过观察发现，受全球文化流动和生产的作用，当今世界出现了新形式的社会想象，在这种新形式的社会想象的影响下，新形式的、跨越民族国家*和其他空间边界的身份认同应运而生。想象是一个难以捉摸的概念，很难对其进行实证研究。个体与群体具有想象新世界和新生活的能力，这表明他们具有能动性*——在特定条件下做出选择和行动的能力。

在全球化研究领域，这一思想主要受到了研究文化的学者的欢迎。对那些强调对全球化过程中的政治、经济模式进行研究的学者来说，阿帕杜莱的研究影响力有限。

局限性

《消失的现代性》最大的问题在于缺少实证数据的支撑。阿帕杜莱所举的例子来自他自己的观察和阅读经历，而不是方法更为科学的实证研究。

该书出版时（1996 年），越来越多的人类学家注意到，全球化进程加剧了人与国家的不平等问题。在他们看来，阿帕杜莱强调人的能动性，强调社会想象的作用，掩盖了全球化对个人和群体在选择方面带来的约束与限制。

---

1. 阿尔君·阿帕杜莱："全球文化经济中的散裂与差异"，《理论、文化与社会》第 7 卷，1990 年 6 月第 2 期，第 295—310 页。
2. 马丁·阿尔布劳："评阿尔君·阿帕杜莱的《消失的现代性：全球化的文化维度》"，《美国社会学杂志》第 103 卷，1998 年 3 月第 5 期，第 1412 页。

8 著作地位

要点 &—⚊

- 在其整个学术生涯中，阿帕杜莱最关注的是提供新的框架和方法，以便更好地对全球化的文化维度进行研究。

- 阿帕杜莱出版了 13 部专著，其中最著名的一部是《消失的现代性》。

- 自 1996 年《消失的现代性》出版以来，阿帕杜莱对他在书中所介绍的概念和方法进行了进一步深入研究。

定位

《消失的现代性：全球化的文化维度》是阿尔君·阿帕杜莱在六年间所撰写论文的结集。该书涵盖了他学术生涯早期最关注的消费*、殖民、迁移*等问题。该书的大部分章节都是他对之前已经发表过的论文进行修改后的版本。该书介绍了文化经由全球经济进行流动的方式，并且为未来的全球化研究指明了方向。

《消失的现代性》一书出版后，阿帕杜莱又出版了两本专著，将其对全球化问题进行的研究不断推进。他撰写了论文《草根全球化与研究的想象力》[1]，作为他主编的《全球化》（2001）[2] 一书的一个章节。在这篇颇具影响力的论文中，他对学术研究与全球化的关系进行了论述。

此外，2006 年，阿帕杜莱出版了《少数人的恐惧：关于愤怒地理学》[3]。此前，他的作品因为没有对全球化的负面效应做出充足论述而受人指摘。在这本书里，他对此进行了回应。这本书主要关注的是种族暴力与全球化之间的关系，在这个问题上，阿帕杜莱对《消失的现代性》介绍过的相关话题进行了更详细的论述。

他最新出版的专著《作为一种文化事实的未来：论全球状况》（2013）[4] 堪称《消失的现代性》一书的姊妹篇，对未来的全球化文化维度研究指出了更为明确的研究方向。这本书与《消失的现代性》一书关注点相似，但是，在这本书中，阿帕杜莱用从孟买贫民窟中获得的一手研究资料支撑了自己的论点。

> "《消失的现代性》一书证明了，在全球化与种族暴力的时代中，跨国*人类学和史学在理论上和方法上做出了多么伟大的贡献。"
> ——D.A. 德·佐萨："评《消失的现代性》"，《国际移民评论》

整合

阿帕杜莱年轻时，作为一名在美国学习的印度学生，他对那些鼓吹现代性*是普世目标或将现代性与某些特定地区联系在一起的理论就非常警惕。随着在人类学研究和区域研究*方面不断深入，对于将文化定位于某一特定地区的研究倾向，阿帕杜莱渐渐持有批判态度。他的学术视角和观点在很大程度上源于他从印度来到美国求学的经历。

阿帕杜莱的著作也受到了这些早期观察与关注点的影响。他试图将现代性描述为一套不同视角的分裂*的体系。他发现，我们需要新的理论和新的方法来理解全球化中的文化变革与人的能动性*。他受到卡尔·马克思的资本主义理论的影响，并对马克思的理论做出了与时俱进的阐述，以更好地适应身份认同极其复杂的全球化时代。他在书中还展示了对全球化的进一步研究可以如何帮助我们理解和解释种族暴力与媒体消费模式等多元化的现象。

随着时间的推移，阿帕杜莱努力对其早期作品中提到过的概念、提出过的研究方法作进一步的明确阐释。此前，阿帕杜莱的作品因其重要思想缺乏实证 * 研究支撑而引发争议。对此，阿帕杜莱最近的作品也进行了回应。他使用了更多以印度为背景的案例来阐发自己的论点。

意义

阿帕杜莱的作品极具影响力。他出版了 13 部专著，发表了 90 余篇文章，但其中最有分量的非《消失的现代性》莫属。

1996 年《消失的现代性》出版时，全球化研究还是一个比较新的领域，人类学研究中也很少有人对文化的全球化层面进行深入的研究。阿帕杜莱在这些领域的开创性研究，为《消失的现代性》一书成为 20 世纪晚期人类学经典著作奠定了坚实的基础。阿帕杜莱后面出版的作品也备受好评，也提出了很多新的概念和新的方法。但是，一提到阿帕杜莱，人们最先想到的还是他在《消失的现代性》中提出的概念——"景观"*（阿帕杜莱发明的术语，表示物品、理念、影像在世界范围内的分布与移动。它一般作为"媒体景观""技术景观""族群景观"等词语的后缀）、散裂 *（断裂或分离点）和社会想象 *。

---

1. 阿尔君·阿帕杜莱："草根全球化与研究的想象力"，《全球化》，阿尔君·阿帕

杜莱编，北卡罗来纳，杜伦：杜克大学出版社，2001 年，第 1—21 页。

2. 阿尔君·阿帕杜莱编：《全球化》，北卡罗来纳，杜伦：杜克大学出版社，2001 年。

3. 阿尔君·阿帕杜莱：《少数人的恐惧：关于愤怒地理学》，北卡罗来纳，杜伦：杜克大学出版社，2006 年。

4. 阿尔君·阿帕杜莱：《作为一种文化事实的未来：论全球状况》，纽约：韦尔素出版公司，2013 年。

.

第三部分：学术影响

9 最初反响

要点 🔑━━

- 对《消失的现代性》一书的批评意见主要集中在以下三个方面：没有实证 * 研究作为基础；夸大了个人与群体的能动性 *；对全球化 * 的前景过于乐观。

- 阿帕杜莱在此后创作的作品中，对全球化的消极影响进行了更充分的论述。但是，他还是更强调个人与群体在建构社会运动的过程中体现出来的能动性。

- 阿帕杜莱的目标受众是所有对全球化问题感兴趣的人。不过，阅读并就《消失的现代性》一书展开热烈讨论的读者多来自人类学 * 和区域研究 * 领域。

批评

在很多文化人类学学者看来，阿尔君·阿帕杜莱的《消失的现代性：全球化的文化维度》缺少民族志 * 田野考察。宾夕法尼亚州立大学的人类学荣休教授 E. 保罗·杜伦伯格 * 就此写道："阿帕杜莱好像完全把民族志和对特定地区的研究抛在了脑后。"[1]

阿帕杜莱也不喜欢说明因果关系（原因和结果直接的关系）。例如，他在书中写到，英国对印度进行殖民 * 统治期间，曾进行人口普查，确定人口数量，把人按种姓（世袭的社会阶层）和宗教关系进行分类。随着时间的推移，这种分类成为群体身份的重要组成部分。不同群体身份之间产生了冲突，并导致了暴力事件的发生。对此，阿帕杜莱并没有说明人口普查这种确定人口数量、对人进行分类的实践行为与南亚当代的种族暴力事件之间的关系，他并没有说明人口普查是否导致了种族暴力，或者说人口普查仅仅是为后来的种族暴力行为创造了一些条件。对于以上问题，因为缺乏实证研究提供的证据，阿帕杜莱无法给出明确的答复。"这本书里充斥着滔滔雄辩的个人意见与观点，缺乏证据的支撑。"[2]

对这本书的第二个批评意见是，阿帕杜莱缺少对全球化的批判。有些人认为，全球化是一个体系，其在结构上依赖于世界范围内的不平等。在他们看来，阿帕杜莱的社会想象*认识不切合实际，全世界人民和群体自由、自主地想象世界和生活，这是不现实的。在他们看来，阿帕杜莱的异质化*（不同社会的文化互相融合、变得愈发多元的过程）观点忽略了政府、金融、劳动等自有其各自规定的内在秩序，这些会对个人和群体的选择加以限制。

《消失的现代性》较少受到政治学或经济学领域学者的引用。一名学者指出："他的写作技巧令人炫目，深受后现代主义者的欢迎。"[3] 后现代主义*学者认为，意义与阐释由各自不同的视角决定，都是不固定的。后现代主义的研究方法在文学批评、人类学等学科中掀起热潮，但是却并不受政治学和经济学领域的青睐。

> 如果阿帕杜莱能够利用他的"景观"理论进行实证的社会历史研究就更妙了。这样一来，他不仅能够展示出全球化视域中不同的文化变革的"新颖性"，更能展示出他的理论的实证价值。
>
> —— 海斯贝特·温克："评《消失的现代性》"，《世界史杂志》

回应

在阿帕杜莱的作品中，全球化是现代世界的关键性特征，其主要特点为全球性文化流动*。他的目标是：用能够反映当下世界实际情况的更好的理论与方法促进全球化研究的发展。因此，他对于全球化的特征是"好"还是"坏"并没有那么关心和关注。

在书中，他描述了全球化如何使社会运动变为可能，以对抗其自身的负面力量。从这个层面上来讲，在全球化的进程中，"机会均等"意为"如果我们日常生活中的问题有了答案，这个答案可以比以往更快地通过互联网、媒体、旅游等科技进步带来的新方法传播给更多人，让他们从中受益"。[4] 在全球化的作用下，问题的答案与问题本身都能以更快的速度进行传播。

阿帕杜莱表示，他是故意忽略因果关系的。他写道："人不可能带着强烈的关于因果关系的前见去看待某一特定的情况。散裂一词描述的正是那种形式。"[5] 不同流动之间存在着矛盾与隔阂，这意味着，任何情况都是由独特的、出人意料的因与果的组合构成。

冲突与共识

阿帕杜莱用个人观察与经历（而不是实证研究）来阐发自己的观点。比方说，他分析了印度人如何把板球这项运动从体现维多利亚时期英国精英的男性魅力转变为体现分裂的[*]、当代的印度男性气质。《消失的现代性》一书缺少实证证明，这其实是有意为之。在书中，阿帕杜莱曾多次表示，后续需要用适当的方法对某一特定论点或案例开展进一步研究。

评论人士曾就阿帕杜莱在《消失的现代性》中体现的全球化观点是否过于积极进行过争论。在之后出版的作品中，阿帕杜莱对此做出了直接回应。在 2006 年出版的《少数人的恐惧：关于愤怒地理学》一书中，阿帕杜莱写道："有些评论人士认为，《消失的现代性》一书把 20 世纪 90 年代初期的全球化描写得太理想化了，没有充分地注意到全球化的阴暗面，如暴力、排外和愈发加剧的不平等。作为对这些声音的回应，同时也出于我个人长期以来的兴趣，我开始研究在我的家乡孟买发生的针对穆斯林的集体暴力行为。"[6]这些研究表明，全球化在激发能动性 * 的同时也滋生了暴力。

---

1. E. 保罗·杜伦伯格："评论：人类学与全球化"，《美国人类学家》第 103 卷，2001 年 6 月第 1 期，第 533 页。

2. 杜伦伯格："评论"第 534 页。

3. 海斯贝特·温克："评阿尔君·阿帕杜莱的《消失的现代性：全球化的文化维度》"，《世界史杂志》第 11 卷，2000 年春第 1 期，第 158 页。

4. 约翰·C. 霍利："后记：阿尔君·阿帕杜莱访谈录"，《后殖民与全球化中的美国人》，利瓦蒂·克里希纳斯瓦米和约翰·C. 霍利编，明尼阿波利斯：明尼苏达大学出版社，2007 年，第 293 页。

5. 阿尔君·阿帕杜莱："关于持久的幻想：阿尔君·阿帕杜莱访谈"，《视点》，2003 年第 34 期，第 45 页。

6. 阿尔君·阿帕杜莱：《少数人的恐惧：关于愤怒地理学》，北卡罗来纳，杜伦：杜克大学出版社，2006 年，第 ix—x 页。

10 后续争议

要点 ⚷

- 阿帕杜莱提出以"景观"*概念作为理解散裂*的出发点,为人类学家*研究全球化的世界中的文化提供了一个新的框架。

- 在过去 20 年里,阿帕杜莱的全球文化流动思想受到了对全球化的文化维度进行研究的大部分学者的欢迎。

- 从社会学到城市规划学,阿帕杜莱的作品在多个领域受到广泛认可。不过,他理论的最忠实的追随者主要是试图对文化和全球化进行深刻理解的人类学家与其他社会科学家。

应用与问题

阿尔君·阿帕杜莱在《消失的现代性:全球化的文化维度》中提出的全球文化流动理论为深入研究全球化的现代特点开了个好头。他认为,全球化的现代特点主要反映在当今世界上难以捉摸的理念、事物与人的运动上,他将其称为"文化流动"。对此,学界人士深表赞同。

在阿帕杜莱的著作中,引用最多的是他关于全球文化流动的五个"景观"的理论:族群景观*、技术景观*、金融景观*、媒体景观*和意识形态景观*。其他学者还以阿帕杜莱的研究为基础,提出了其他的重要"景观",或者对这五种"景观"在特定地点出现的方式进行了检视与研究。

阿帕杜莱强调社会想象*的力量,对我们理解在全球化文化力量的作用下个人与群体的能动性*有着巨大而深远的意义。他对想象的研究植根于悠久的学术传统中，受到了从社会学研究前驱学者爱米尔·杜尔凯姆*、马克斯·韦伯*到法国社会学家与人类学家皮埃尔·布尔迪厄*再到民族主义学者本尼迪克特·安德森等人的影响。因此，阿帕杜莱的学术地位、学术影响力主要来自他创新提出的"景观"理论，而非其想象理论。

> "现在，很少能看到完全没有受到全球散裂理论影响的研究生……从这个角度上说，阿帕杜莱的文章可以说是学术上的分水岭。"
>
> —— 彼得·梅特卡夫："全球'散裂'与人类学的'场地'"，
> 《文化人类学》

思想流派

《消失的现代性》是全球化研究领域的重要著作。据谷歌学术统计，该书迄今已经被引用了近两万次。许多作家、学者、思想家都深受其影响。

该书中蕴含的思想涵盖范围颇广，但论述却不甚明晰，可见，这本书并不企图开创学术上的新传统，而是希望能够鼓舞更多的学者在现有的文化研究、文化交流研究方法上进行创新。《消失的现代性》是"一个学术上同时也是个人层面上的长期项目"的一部分，"该项目旨在寻找到新的方法，让全世界的穷人、无家可归者、弱者、社会边缘人士等最需要全球化但同时也最受全球化之苦的人们真正享受到全球化能够带来的福祉"[1]。此后，在对印度孟买的贫民窟进行了长期跟踪研究后，阿帕杜莱写到了城市规划可以如何对贫民窟里的穷苦居民的想象与期待进行回应。

当代研究

    《消失的现代性》出版二十多年来，阿帕杜莱的思想和理论深刻影响了大部分希望对当今全球化世界中的文化加强理解、对特定社群或地区的社会变革加以阐释的学者。

    有的学者在阿帕杜莱理论的基础上，在他提出的五个"景观"之外提出了新的"景观"。例如，英国的马丁·阿尔布劳*等社会学家又提出了"社会景观"*这一概念，以表示人际关系和社交网络的流动。阿尔布劳写道："我们认为，'景观'这个词为实证的社会研究打开了新的研究视角，使其突破传统的社会和社群理念，更好地对本土/全球之间的关系进行研究。"[2]

    其他学者对五种"景观"在特定地区的表现方式进行了研究。弗吉尼亚大学的人类学荣休教授彼得·梅特卡夫*与其他人类学家发现，"景观"观念为他们奠定了坚实的基础，帮助他们更好地理解了过去几十年里他们研究的族群所面临的深刻而快速的变革。梅特卡夫在其对婆罗洲的研究论文中写道："应用了阿帕杜莱提出的研究模型后，我清楚地认识到，我所认识的那个 70 年代的上游世界已经在触角极长、威力巨大的社会力量的作用下土崩瓦解了。这些社会力量不会一致行动，甚至也不会互相竞争，它们体现出来的是一种不顾一切的贪婪。"[3]

---

1. 阿尔君·阿帕杜莱：《少数人的恐惧：关于愤怒地理学》，北卡罗来纳，杜伦：杜

克大学出版社，2006 年，第 xi 页。

2. 马丁·阿尔布劳："评阿尔君·阿帕杜莱的《消失的现代性：全球化的文化维度》"，《美国社会学杂志》第 103 卷，1998 年 3 月第 5 期，第 1412 页。

3. 彼得·梅特卡夫："全球'散裂'与人类学的'场地'"，《文化人类学》第 16 卷，第 2 期，第 173 页。

11 当代印迹

要点 ⚷━

- 出版 20 年来，《消失的现代性》一书已经成为全球化 * 研究的人类学 * 经典。

- 阿帕杜莱认为，全球化研究一定要在经济、政治维度之外不忘涵盖文化维度。

- 《消失的现代性》一书从整体上来说没有受到经济学领域的重视。

地位

阿尔君·阿帕杜莱出版《消失的现代性：全球化的文化维度》时，全球化研究还是一个新的学术领域。这本书可以看作是阿帕杜莱与其他全球化研究学者之间的一种对话。书的副标题表明，这本书旨在对全球化的文化维度进行探索与研究。

阿帕杜莱提醒人类学家，在全球化影响下，人与文化实践活动表现出了去国土化 * 特征，因此，应当对文化研究的方法与理论进行重新思考。他提出了一个新的、建立在全球文化流动的五个"景观" * （族群景观 *、技术景观 *、金融景观 *、媒体景观 * 和意识形态景观 * ）与它们之间的"散裂"（分离点）基础上的研究框架。

在人类学家看来，这本书注定要成为经典，特别是其中的第二章《全球文化经济中的散裂与差异》。过去 20 年来，在对文化的全球化元素进行研究的人类学著作、论文中，大部分都引用了该书的观点。

该书对不同学科的研究都能有所助益，但是，对于其对全球化文化维度的重要性的强调，政治学家与经济学家却并不怎么买账。特别是经济学家，他们对全球化的研究多从理性的、自上而下的学术视角出发，对文化维度的兴趣仅存在于用它解释个人与群体消费习惯。

> "人类学家实质上已经把对未来的研究事务主盘交给了经济学。"
>
> —— 阿尔君·阿帕杜莱："关于持久的幻想：阿尔君·
> 阿帕杜莱访谈"，《视点》

互动

在阿帕杜莱看来，对全球化经济的分析中，文化起着至关重要的作用，原因有三。

一、在对全球化的经济分析中，当下的全球化往往被看作为一个顺利、流畅的过程，而文化分析却能帮助我们注意到全球化过程中的不稳定、多元化与差异性。

二、经济分析往往会做出关于同质化＊的预测，认为在全球化的作用下，整个世界正变得越来越小，越来越相像。但是，与此相反的是，文化分析却往往强调异质化＊——人与理念在全球范围内流动，促进了社会想象的出现，由此产生了新的或多元混杂的文化形式。

三、经济分析往往缺乏历史的视角，过于关注个人的活动，没有充分认识到个人作为群体社会的一部分，深受国家历史、地域因素、身份认同等因素的影响。文化分析可以帮助人们对当代全球化的世界进行深入研究，"回顾过去"，认清当下社会活动中蕴含的历史因素。

阿帕杜莱并不指责经济学家忽视了文化。他更希望的是鼓励人类学家在进行经济分析的过程中考虑文化因素。

持续争议

关于研究中的经济与文化视角能否调和，学者们一直有所争论。比如，加州大学伯克利分校的经济学家普兰纳布·巴德汉*与伊莎·雷*就认为，经济学与人类学在理论上与方法上背道而驰，"一般都被看作社会科学序列中的两极"[1]。其中，两者间最大的差别就是自主性（经济学）与嵌入性（人类学）之间的差异。也就是说，经济学分析往往把个人看作相对独立的主体，个人可以在各种可能性中进行自主选择；而人类学家认为，个人深深嵌入在文化中，个人的选择受到了社会环境的制约。

经济学与人类学之间的另一个关键区别是结果（经济学）与过程（人类学）之间的差异。经济学寻求的是全球结构、政治、事件产生的结果，而人类学关注的是复杂的关系与使结果产生的事件本身。相应地，两者之间的第三个区别是简约法*（经济学家喜欢对研究对象进行简单的、线性的分析）与复杂性（人类学家旨在描述社会的错综复杂）之间的差别。

关于全球化，经济学家和人类学家提出的问题是完全不同的，试图解答的问题也是完全不同的。尽管阿尔君·阿帕杜莱、克利福德·格尔茨*、玛丽·道格拉斯*等人类学家试着与经济学家一起开展研究，但因为这两个学科之间的差异实在是过于巨大，他们将经济学与人类学结合起来的尝试最终都以失败而告终。

　　但是，也有部分经济学家已经注意到，经济学研究项目里缺乏文化分析。哈佛大学的经济学教授阿马蒂亚·森*指出："在对发展进行分析的过程中，我们需要对发展的文化维度进行细致审慎的研究。"[2] 文化可以帮助人们更好地理解为发展项目奠定基础或对发展项目的成功造成阻碍的政治过程。

---

1. 普兰纳布·巴德汉和伊莎·雷："经济学与人类学的方法论"，《Q 平方工作论文》之 17，多伦多大学国际研究中心，2006 年 2 月，第 1 页。
2. 阿马蒂亚·森："文化如何要紧？"，《文化与公共行为》，维瓦扬德拉·饶和迈克尔·沃尔顿编，斯坦福：斯坦福大学出版社，2004 年，第 37 页。

12 未来展望

要点 🔑

- 阿尔君·阿帕杜莱的研究将鼓舞着人类学家以及其他社会科学研究者不断前进。

- 如果反全球化社会运动不断发展壮大，经济学专家和政治学专家将对这本书中强调的全球化的文化维度引起足够的重视。

- 在对全球化的人类学研究中，学者们引用最多的就是《消失的现代性》，特别是其中的第二章《全球文化经济中的散裂与差异》。

潜力

阿尔君·阿帕杜莱在《消失的现代性：全球化的文化维度》中介绍了在当今全球化的背景下人类学家和其他领域的学者应该如何开展学术研究。阿帕杜莱还介绍了一些具有重要意义的研究方法，助力全球化研究的不断深入与发展。

尽管有批评人士指出阿帕杜莱提出的问题远远多于他回答的问题，但是，这也可以算是这本书在推动后续研究方面具有的深远意义。阿帕杜莱对读者们提出了非常明确的建议，指导他们在各自的研究中应用自己的理论和思想。

《消失的现代性》注定是一部人类学经典之作。20世纪末，人类学家正苦苦寻求将现代性*与全球化融入到文化研究中的方法，这本书的出版对人类学学科的发展产生了决定性的影响。阿帕杜莱强调文化形式的异质化*，在这一思想的指引下，人类学家将全球的与本土的文化联系在了一起。

对于全球化是如何催生并加剧了当今的种族暴力的,《消失的现代性》以及阿帕杜莱此后出版的作品都引起了学术界的相关讨论。

> "现在民族志的任务是解开如下难题:在全球化的、去国土化的世界中,地方性作为一种生命经验有着怎样的本质?"
>
> —— 阿尔君・阿帕杜莱:《消失的现代性:全球化的文化维度》

未来方向

一些人类学家深受阿帕杜莱"景观"理论的影响,并在此基础上不断深入拓展。他们发现了在全球文化流动结合 * 和散裂 * 时产生的其他"景观"。如英国学者马丁・阿尔布劳 * 等社会学家又提出了"社会景观" * 这一概念,作为全球文化流动 * 的第六个维度。[1] 社会景观将一个社群或地区中个人的人际关系与社交网络组织了起来。

阿帕杜莱的批评者也会使用他发明的术语,指出还有很多其他阿帕杜莱未提及的"景观",以此证明其理论的局限性。例如,荷兰世界史专家海斯贝特・温克指出,阿帕杜莱遗漏了与科学以及环境相关的"景观"。[2] 其实,这恰恰证明了,即使批评人士们对《消失的现代性》提出的观点并不完全赞同,但是不得不承认这本书具有巨大的学术潜力,对开拓新的研究方向具有重要意义。

阿帕杜莱希望引导政治学、经济学等领域的研究人员关注全球化中的文化维度。但是整体而言,这两个领域的研究者尚未意识到文化在其研究中的重要性。不过阿帕杜莱预测,与人权、妇女权益、社会公平等全球问题相关的跨国 * 社会运动正在兴起。随着这些运动的壮大,越来越多研究全球化的学者会接受文化的重要性。

小结

　　在《消失的现代性》一书中，阿帕杜莱指出，学者们应该深入认识族群景观*（人）、技术景观*（技术）、金融景观*（钱）、媒体景观*（影像）、意识形态景观*（社会形态）这五种"景观"或者全球文化流动的结合与散裂，不断推进全球化文化维度的研究。他最关注的是大规模迁移和电子媒体，因为，这两大重要的过程使人和理念在世界范围内移动。这些过程引发了散裂，在此身份、理念、视角发生碰撞。

　　该书并未以阿帕杜莱自己的实证*研究为基础。但是，这本书为未来如何在去国土化*与跨国*行为盛行的世界中进行"景观"研究提供了许多好的思路与方法。阿帕杜莱建议人类学家们借鉴文化研究*的方法，使民族志*研究能够真正反映出全球化背景下人的生活与理念如何跨越时空限制联系在了一起。

　　《消失的现代性》一书问世时，大部分学者对全球化的关注都局限于全球化如何剥夺了人的权力。阿帕杜莱的全球化理论却描绘了一幅更为复杂的图景，因为，在全球化的结构与过程中，人还有能动性*。人与理念在世界范围内流动、碰撞，产生了社会想象*，人们能够想象新的世界与新的生活。这种想象源自许多不同的方面，如对祖国的怀恋、大众媒体、个人经历。这种想象具有强大的驱动力量，使全球化呈现出了积极与消极的面貌。

　　具有讽刺意味的是，全球化一方面加深了人与理念之间的隔阂，另一方面也消融了这种隔阂。在这样的历史背景下，阿帕杜莱的思想将继续指导社会科学家们对人、文化、世界体系等进行不断深入的研究。

1. 马丁·阿尔布劳：《全球时代：超越现代性的国家与社会》，加利福尼亚，斯坦福：斯坦福大学出版社，1996 年。
2. 海斯贝特·温克："评阿尔君·阿帕杜莱的《消失的现代性：全球化的文化维度》"，《世界史杂志》第 11 卷，2000 年春第 1 期，第 158 页。

术语表

1. **能动性**：人在特定条件下做出选择和行动的能力。

2. **人类学**：对人类的行为和实践活动进行的系统研究。

3. **区域研究**：对某一特定地理地区或民族地区进行的跨学科研究。

4. **殖民**：一个国家被另一个国家统治、剥削的历史时期。

5. **比较政治学**：对不同国家或不同时代的政治、机构、分歧进行比较的学术研究方法。

6. **结合**：联结与相会点。

7. **中心国家**：根据世界体系理论，发达国家处于全球资本主义经济的中心地位。

8. **克里奥尔化**：克里奥尔文化的产生过程——在新世界里两种或多种语言结合在一起产生一种新的文化。在人类学领域，这个词指的是不同文化形式和文化身份有意地结合在一起的过程。

9. **文化帝国主义**：一个更加强大的社会的文化形式压倒甚至取代弱小社会的文化形式的过程。这个词语常被用来指称美国文化在世界范围内的盛行。

10. **文化主义**：用独特的文化身份来使自己与其他群体区别开来，特别是在民族国家的层面上。

11. **文化研究**：20世纪中叶在英国学术界兴起的跨学科研究，旨在对文化理念本身及文化理念如何产生、定义、使用进行分析。文化研究对人类学的研究方法有所借鉴，但在文化研究看来，文化并不是存在于人类生活中的一个事实，而是特定时间、特定地点在权力和控制的作用下形成的一种理念。

12. **去国土化**：对于与本土、地域、国家身份或机制相关的空间界限进行的解构。

13. **流离**：有相同的地理来源以及身份认同（与历史相关）的分散的人群。

14. **散裂**：断裂或分离点。

15. **电子媒体**：媒体的生产和国际传播技术，例如卫星电视和互联网。

16. **实证**：指的是基于直接经历或观察的研究或数据。

17. **民族志**：文化人类学家为了理解文化采取的一种研究方法，一般是通过在某一特定地区进行长期田野调查开展的。这个术语也可以用来指通过这种研究方法得出的成果，比方说一本书或一部电影。

18. **族群景观**：阿帕杜莱提出的术语，指的是世界范围内的人口分布，强调的是在全球范围内活动的移民、游客等。

19. **金融景观**：阿帕杜莱用来表示在全球范围内快速移动的金钱的分布与流动的术语。

20. **分裂的**：分裂成碎片。在身份认同方面，这个词指的是身份具有复杂性，每个个体的身份都有多种不同成分构成。

21. **法兰克福学派**：20世纪早期到20世纪中叶在德国法兰克福大学社会研究中心兴起的社会理论和哲学学派。该学派吸收了经济学家、政治哲学家卡尔·马克思（以对作为历史推动力的阶级斗争进行分析和对资本主义进行批判而著称）的理论，对资本主义和社会发展的过程进行了批判。

22. **地理学家**：致力于系统研究世界的自然特征以及这些自然特征与人口分布、资源分布等因素之间的关系的人。

23. **全球文化流动**：全球化带来的全球文化维度或领域的活动。

24. **全球家园**：人类学家乌尔夫·翰纳兹提出的一个词，指的是人们的观念不再植根并局限于一个地区，而是在世界范围内流动。"家园"指的是人们定居并视为永久的家的地方。

25. **全球化**：世界正愈发迅猛地在经济、政治、文化领域互联互通的过程。

26. **异质化**：不同社会的文化互相融合、变得愈发多元的过程。

27. **同质化**：不同社会的文化面貌变得愈发相似的过程。

28. **意识形态景观**：阿帕杜莱提出的术语，用来指称与民族或国家的意识形态相关的不断变化的全球政治形象景观。

29. **想象的共同体**：由民族主义学者本尼迪克特·安德森提出的概念，阐述了一个群体（如一个国家）如何在其成员彼此之间无任何直接联系互动的情况下产生认同感。

30. **麦克阿瑟学者**：获得麦克阿瑟学术奖金的学者，该奖金以五年为期，由麦克阿瑟基金会颁发给具有非凡创造性的杰出人士。

31. **媒体景观**：阿帕杜莱提出的术语，指的是为观者想象自己和想象世界提供素材的在世界范围内移动的视觉描述景观。

32. **迁移**：指的是或被迫或自愿进行的个人或群体从一个地方到另一个地方的迁移。

33. **现代性**：学者们用这个词指 19 世纪后期到 20 世纪中叶这段时间以及在此期间技术、经济、政治上的发展。

34. **现代化理论**：20 世纪 50 年代和 60 年代在美国社会学领域兴起的理论流派，旨在研究和解释在 20 世纪中叶传统社会如何不断发展，在技术、经济、政治和其他各领域取得与西方社会相应的进展。

35. **民族主义**：一种坚信对民族或民族国家的认同或兴趣具有重要意义的意识形态。

36. **民族国家**：把对主权国家（国家）的控制与民族或文化身份联系到一起的政治实体。

37. **简约法**：这里指的是为大量的观察寻求最简单的解释的研究。

38. **边缘国家**：根据世界体系理论，发展中国家处于全球资本主义经济的边缘位置。

39. **后殖民**：一个社会对另一个社会殖民结束之后的阶段。这个词也可以指对殖民主义的后续影响进行研究的学术视角。

40. **后现代**：20 世纪晚期在文学批评、人类学以及其他批判普遍真理这一理念的学科中掀起的一股潮流。对后现代主义学者来说，意义与阐释都是不固定的，是由各自不同的视角决定的。

41. **后民族**：指的是作为实体的民族国家不复存在或力量削弱的时间或状态。

42. **原始的**：一种基于共同的生物学本质或亲缘关系带来的强烈情感做出的种族身份界定。

43. **印刷资本主义**：由民族主义学者本尼迪克特·安德森提出的概念，指的是受众使用同一种语言的报纸、杂志、书籍的生产、传播和消费。

44. **断裂**：破裂。在阿帕杜莱看来，断裂是当下文化、身份、全球文化流动的特性，人与观念都脱离其原生地，以全新的方式进行彼此间的交流。

45. **"景观"**：阿帕杜莱发明的术语，表示物品、理念、影响在世界范围内的分布与移动。它一般作为"媒体景观""技术景观""族群景观"等词语的后缀。

46. **社会想象**：一种有组织的社会实践，通过这种社会想象，个人与社会群体构想了理想的生活形式，并努力实现这种新的可能性。在阿帕杜莱看来，社会想象是新的全球秩序的重要组成部分。

47. **社会学**：对人类社会的历史、特性与功能进行的系统研究。

48. **社会景观**：马丁·阿尔布罗及其同事受阿帕杜莱的启发发明的概念，用来描述社交网络和人际关系的分布与流动。

49. **主体性**：在阿帕杜莱看来，由文化塑造的对个人自我和个人经历的意识和认识。

50. **技术景观**：阿帕杜莱用来表示全球技术分布与移动的术语。

51. **跨国**：跨越民族国家的边界进行移动和操作。

52. **世界体系理论**：美国社会学家伊曼纽尔·沃勒斯坦提出的一系列理论，根据世界上各个国家与全球资本主义经济之间的关系，将它们分为"中心国家""半边缘国家""边缘国家"。

人名表

1. 马丁·阿尔布劳（1937年生），英国社会学家，主要研究领域是全球化与社会变化。

2. 本尼迪克特·安德森（1936年生），美国知名学者，康纳尔大学国际研究荣休教授。他最出名的是民族主义研究和想象的共同体理论。

3. 普兰纳布·巴德汉（1939年生），加州大学伯克利分校的经济学教授。他主要的研究领域是贸易经济学、国际发展、贫穷国家的农村体制。

4. 弗朗兹·博厄斯（1858—1942），德裔美国人类学教授，在哥伦比亚大学创立了美国第一个人类学系。他推崇历史特殊论以及文化相对论的研究范式（概念模型与解释框架），创立了至今仍在美国文化人类学领域广泛使用的参与观察法。

5. 皮埃尔·布尔迪厄（1930—2002），法国社会学家、哲学家、人类学家。在人类学领域，他最重要的贡献是提出了"习惯"概念，用来表示个人身上体现的一套文化倾向。

6. 卡罗尔·布雷肯里奇（1942—2009），美国印度历史学家，阿尔君·阿帕杜莱的妻子。她研究的主要方向是文化理论和殖民主义。她和阿帕杜莱一起创办了学术期刊《公众文化》，该刊物是全球化研究和跨国主义研究领域的核心刊物。

7. 玛丽·道格拉斯（1921—2007），英国人类学家，其主要研究方向为象征人类学（对与宗教与食物相关的社会象征符号进行的研究）。

8. 爱米尔·杜尔凯姆（1858—1917），法国社会学家，现代社会科学理论的先驱学者，社会学学科创建者。他提出的社会团结与集体良知理论至今仍影响深远。

9. E.保罗·杜伦伯格，宾夕法尼亚州立大学的人类学荣休教授。他的主要学术贡献在于其对全球化进行的人类学研究，特别是关于劳动的研究。

10. **克利福德·格尔茨**（1926—2006），美国普林斯顿高等科学研究所人类学教授。美国历史上最受欢迎的人类学家之一，象征人类学的提出者，创作了多部关于宗教、经济学、人类学研究方法的专著。

11. **乌尔夫·翰纳兹**（1942年生），瑞典斯德哥尔摩大学的荣休教授。他最著名的是对文化和全球化的研究。

12. **卡尔·马克思**（1818—1883），生于德国普鲁士的哲学家和经济学家。他创作的关于资本主义、共产主义、历史变化本质的作品历久弥新。

13. **彼得·梅特卡夫**，弗吉尼亚大学的人类学荣休教授，曾出版过比较宗教与东南亚研究方面的著作。

14. **海斯贝特·温克**，荷兰伊拉斯姆斯历史、文化与传播学院的非洲与南亚史副教授。他曾经发表过关于印度历史和全球化的论文。

15. **伊莎·雷**，加州大学伯克利分校的能源与资源教授。她的主要研究领域包括水资源、发展、性别问题。

16. **阿马蒂亚·森**（1933年生），印度经济学家、哲学家，目前在哈佛大学担任教授。他的著作主要聚焦发展问题，读者既涵盖了学者，也包括了普通读者。因其在福利经济学领域的突出贡献，1998年他获得了诺贝尔经济学奖。

17. **约翰·汤姆林森**，英国诺丁汉特伦特大学英国文化与传媒项目的文化社会学荣休教授。他写过关于全球化与文化的著作，并在国家组织和包括联合国教科文组织在内的国际组织担任顾问。

18. **伊曼纽尔·沃勒斯坦**（1930年生），美国社会学家，创立了世界体系理论，研究全球资本主义经济中各国间的不平等关系。

19. **马克斯·韦伯**（1864—1920），德国哲学家，在社会理论领域有突出贡献，是社会学这一学科的创始元老级人物。他在学术上的最大贡献是对西方工业国家的经济和政治进行的研究。

WAYS IN TO THE TEXT

- Arjun Appadurai was born in India in 1949. In 1967, he moved to the United States, where he has lived and worked ever since. His experiences of living in India and the United States informed his ideas about culture and globalization* (the study of the cultural and social effects of a globally connected world).

- Appadurai's approach in *Modernity at Large* is unique in that, whereas most previous accounts of globalization focused on its economic or political aspects, Appadurai concentrates on people, culture, and ideas.

- *Modernity at Large* remains a key text for anthropologists* and geographers* who are trying to make sense of globalization. (Anthropologists are engaged in the systematic study of the beliefs and practices of the world's peoples; geographers study the world's physical features and the relationship between them and factors such as the distribution of populations and resources.)

Who Is Arjun Appadurai?

Arjun Appadurai, the author of *Modernity at Large: Cultural Dimensions of Globalization* (1996), was born in 1949 and grew up in Mumbai, India. He sometimes discusses his childhood in his work, referring to his early subjectivity*—a term he uses to refer to a sense of self shaped through culture—as "postcolonial."* India was a British colony between 1858 and 1947 (that is, ruled and exploited by Britain), and British cultural influences still dominated India when Appadurai was a child. These influences shaped his subjectivity, as did the American cultural influences that he encountered later in his life.

Appadurai left India for the United States in 1967 and obtained a PhD from the University of Chicago in 1976. His studies focused on modernization: the technological, economic, political, and general advances associated with Western societies during the mid-twentieth century.

Since the age of 18, Appadurai has traveled back and forth between India and the United States. His work theorizes the movement of people and ideas across borders and regions. He argues that the way different people experience modernity*—the period during and following modernization—depends on their perspective. The world may look different to people living in India and the United States, but they are all experiencing modernity.

Appadurai wrote *Modernity at Large* between 1990 and 1996. At that time, he was working as codirector of the Center for Transnational* Cultural Studies at the University of Pennsylvania. He later moved to the University of Chicago, and is currently at New York University.

What Does *Modernity at Large* Say?

Modernity at Large lays out an innovative framework for studying globalization in relation to modernity. According to Appadurai, Western social science has theorized modernity as a sudden break between past and present. He describes several problematic features of this theory. First, modernization theory* (an approach developed in the field of sociology* in the United States during the 1950s and 1960s to explain how traditional societies could develop and achieve the technological, economic, political, and other kinds of advances associated with Western societies during the mid-twentieth century) implies that "the West" is modern and "the rest" need help to achieve modernity. Second, according to conventional accounts, globalization always leads to homogenization* (i.e. societies are bound to look more like each other as they evolve toward a Western version of modernity). Appadurai disagrees, arguing that globalization and related processes of deterritorialization* (people and things becoming less tied to their places of origin) mean that modernization is not uniformly progressive and homogenizing.

Appadurai believes that the globalized world can be better understood through his own theory of rupture,* that is, the tendency of people and ideas to break away from their point of origin. He suggests that scholars follow him in examining new types of "global cultural flows"* that circulate the world. Migration* (the movement of people from one place to another) and electronic media* (technologies that proliferate images and ideas) are two of the most important flows. Appadurai saw them as major forces of cultural change, especially in the two decades before publication of the book. These flows produce a world full of diverse identities.

Together, the flows of people and images allow "the work of the imagination." For Appadurai, imagination "has become a part of the quotidian [everyday] mental work of ordinary people in many societies."[1] People move around the world and consume mass media, which enables them to imagine new lives and new worlds. This is an important part of modern subjectivity: people are imagining modernity into being, by imagining themselves as modern.

The modern social imagination* (an organized field of social practices through which individuals and communities picture and work toward new possibilities for how they want to live) disrupts institutions that were previously regarded as the hallmarks of modernity. One of these is the nation-state.* Many people now live in diasporas,* communities that originated in a particular place but are now spread out around the world. No matter what nation-state they may now live in, members of a diaspora continue to imagine their homeland. They do so in part through consuming mass-media images that reinforce their diasporic identity. This is one example of how the world is becoming "postnational."*

In *Modernity at Large*, Appadurai calls on anthropologists to develop new theories and methods for studying the world in its state of flux. These should address how global cultural flows work, and take into account how the social imagination produces new forms of subjectivity.

Modernity at Large made Appadurai's name as an anthropologist of globalization. It has had a lasting impact on the field of anthropology and is set to become a classic in the field. Google Scholar records almost 20,000 citations of the book.

Why Does *Modernity at Large* Matter?

Appadurai published *Modernity at Large* in 1996 when anthropologists, accustomed to focusing on small communities living in one place, were struggling to develop new research methods that reflected the globalized world. Appadurai argued that anthropological methods should recognize that everywhere is now globally connected. He suggested that scholars examine global flows such as migration and electronic media.

Appadurai's book convinced anthropologists, who were used to treating their objects of study as fixed, to study culture in flux. It suggested that they could achieve this by using models from the field of cultural studies. Many have taken up Appadurai's challenge and expanded their understanding of culture to include the effects of globalization.

Anthropologists of globalization have endeavored to find a balance between two approaches. One emphasizes how globalization homogenizes the world through cultural imperialism,* a process in which the cultural forms of a more powerful society dominate or replace the cultural forms of a less powerful one. The other approach emphasizes the opposite: how globalization makes the world more diverse in character. Migration and media, for example, are constantly producing new or hybrid cultural forms. Appadurai's text argues in favor of this second position.

Other anthropologists argue that the most important aspect of globalization is its tendency to create poverty, despair, and displacement. Although Appadurai also reflects on the violent aspects of globalization, *Modernity at Large* ends on an optimistic note. Global cultural flows enable grassroots social movements that can combat globalization's harsh effects. (Grassroots is a term that describes social movements organized from the bottom up, through the actions of members rather than leaders.)

The book has been less convincing for people working in

globalization studies who have continued to focus more on the economic and political aspects of globalization.

---

1. Arjun Appadurai, *Modernity at Large: Cultural Dimensions of Globalization* (Minneapolis: University of Minnesota Press, 1996), 5.

SECTION 1
INFLUENCES

MODULE 1
THE AUTHOR AND THE
HISTORICAL CONTEXT

KEY POINTS

• *Modernity at Large* is a key text in the anthropology* of globalization* and has been cited on Google Scholar almost 20,000 times.

• Arjun Appadurai was born and brought up in India and has spent his adult life in the United States. This has influenced his theory that people and ideas are no longer linked to fixed locales, or areas.

• Appadurai wrote *Modernity at Large* for a broad audience in fields such as anthropology, area studies* (the interdisciplinary study of a particular geographical or national region) and globalization studies. The book coined many important terms still used by anthropologists.

Why Read This Text?

In his 1996 book *Modernity at Large:Cultural Dimensions of Globalization*, Arjun Appadurai—currently Goddard Professor in Media, Culture, and Communication at New York University— argues for a new theoretical framework, or working methodology, based on the concept of global cultural flows* (the movement around the world of dimensions or aspects of culture, set in motion by globalization). This concept is intended to help the study of culture in a modern, globalized world.

Appadurai argues that, while previous scholarship analyzed culture as linked to a particular locale, this is no longer useful.

Appadurai's framework encourages the study of how ideas, things, and people move around the world in global cultural flows, such as migration* (people moving to live in different countries from the ones in which they were born) and electronic media* (the internet, TV, movies, and so on).

Migration and mass media affect the social imagination*— the ways in which people collectively imagine their lives and their worlds. This leads to new possibilities in how people identify themselves.

Appadurai's insights provided important new directions for anthropologists who were looking for methods and theories to understand culture in a globalized world. The book also encouraged people studying globalization to consider the central importance of cultural aspects of this phenomenon.

> *"The story of mass migrations (voluntary and forced) is hardly a new feature of human history. But when it is juxtaposed with the rapid flow of mass-mediated images, scripts, and sensations, we have a new order of instability in the production of modern subjectivities."*
>
> —— Arjun Appadurai, *Modernity at Large: Cultural Dimensions of Globalization*

Author's Life

Appadurai was born in 1949 and grew up in Mumbai, India, where his subjectivity,* or sense of self, was greatly affected by the culture that surrounded him: the aftereffects of the British colonization of India, as well as American media and pop culture. He moved to the United States to attend college in 1967 and has been there ever since. Appadurai was married to Carol Breckenridge,* an American historian of India. His lifetime of travel back and forth between these two places helped him develop his insights into the global flow of people and ideas.

Appadurai received his PhD from the University of Chicago in 1976 and has held appointments at a number of prestigious American institutions, including Yale, Pennsylvania, Chicago, Princeton, and New York universities.

Appadurai uses examples from his personal life to illustrate his ideas. He describes a trip to India with his wife and 11-year-old son, in which the boy encountered "many webs of shifting biography"[1]—different ways of relating to tradition, family, and personal identity—among family members with personal and professional ties in India, the United States, and elsewhere.

For Appadurai, the multiple threads that make up people's identities should be the focus of a new kind of ethnography.* Ethnography describes both the method of research and the work produced by cultural anthropologists. Ethnographies have typically been produced through long-term involvement with a locale, observing and participating in the lives of the people who live there. Appadurai argues for ethnographic research that "focuses on the unyoking of imagination from place."[2] As people move around the world, living and working in different locations, how they imagine and experience their lives changes. They define themselves partly through the people and ideas they encounter, rather than simply through their place of origin.

Author's Background

Appadurai grew up in the 1950s and 1960s. His country of origin, India, was one of many facing the postcolonial* task of building a national and cultural identity after gaining independence. Although British colonialism ended in India in 1947, the country was still dominated by British cultural influences during Appadurai's childhood. However, this was changing quickly as a new postcolonial Indian identity asserted itself.

The quest for a unified Indian identity was fragmented* by the diversity of ethnic and religious identities among the Indian population, with some of these communities stretching across the borders of India into other countries. The end of colonial rule opened up new possibilities for self-determination, so the postcolonial period in South Asia was characterized by conflict between communities and nations seeking political power—and other kinds of power, too—within shifting geopolitical boundaries.

When Appadurai arrived in the United States in 1967, he studied anthropology, area studies, and "that triumphal form of modernization theory* that was still a secure article of Americanism in a bipolar world."[3] Modernization theory was developed by American sociologists* (scholars of the nature, formations, and history of society) during the 1950s and 1960s to explain how traditional societies could develop the technological, economic, political, and other advantages that were at that time concentrated in Western countries. The United States was in the midst of the

Cold War, a period of political and military tension between Western countries and the Soviet Union and nations aligned to it. Scholars and ordinary Americans alike saw the United States as the perfect example of modernity,* particularly in contrast with the Soviet Union, which they considered backward and repressive.

Appadurai's early experiences in India and the United States have shaped his intellectual career. *Modernity at Large* responds to American social science theories of modernity and modernization—for example, that modernity was a universally desirable result of Western progress—while the book's discussions of identity and ethnic violence draw on examples from postcolonial India. The book reflects Appadurai's position as somebody whose work and life draw on ideas and images from multiple communities.

---

1. Arjun Appadurai, *Modernity at Large: Cultural Dimensions of Globalization* (Minneapolis: University of Minnesota Press, 1996), 57.

2. Appadurai, *Modernity at Large*, 58.

3. Appadurai, *Modernity at Large*, 2.

MODULE 2
ACADEMIC CONTEXT

KEY POINTS

- Cultural anthropology* studies the cultural aspects of human existence.

- Although Appadurai is a cultural anthropologist, *Modernity at Large* mainly relies upon the work of theorists outside his own discipline, including the political scientist and historian Benedict Anderson,* who developed a theory of the use of imagination to build community.

- Appadurai suggests that anthropologists can learn from the approach of cultural studies.*

The Work in Its Context

Arjun Appadurai's *Modernity at Large: Cultural Dimensions of Globalization* challenges the methods that American anthropologists were using at the time of writing (1990 to 1996). The German American scholar Franz Boas* is widely credited with being the father of American anthropology. He was uninterested in universal theories of human culture, and preferred long-term ethnographic* research in a particular locale and collecting descriptive empirical* data (that is, collecting verifiable information through observation and interviews, over a long period).

In contrast with Boas and other American anthropologists, Appadurai called for ethnographic research that addressed the global as well as the local. His work was influenced by other anthropologists: for example, studies in the 1970s and 1980s exploring how societies were linked by trade and other international flows.

Modernity at Large acknowledges that societies have been interacting with each other for a long time through trade and other means. However, these interactions intensified in the 1980s and 1990s because transportation and communication became significantly cheaper than before. People and ideas were able to move rapidly around the world, which led to them becoming disconnected from particular locales. Appadurai suggests that anthropology must develop new theories and methods to account for global cultural flows* and how these flows affect particular places.

> "[A] genuinely cosmopolitan ethnographic practice requires an interpretation of the terrain of cultural studies in the United States today and of the status of anthropology within such a terrain."
>
> —— Arjun Appadurai, *Modernity at Large: Cultural Dimensions of Globalization*

Overview of the Field

Although Appadurai is writing with an audience of anthropologists in mind, his work draws mostly upon scholars outside the field of anthropology. For example,he was influenced byWorld Systems Theory,* which aims to describe how and why money, resources, and power are distributed globally. World Systems Theorists such as the US sociologist Immanuel Wallerstein* laid out the structure of the relationships between "core"* (developed) and "periphery"* (developing) nations to analyze global political and economic inequalities.

Some anthropologists, like Appadurai, were influenced by the theories of the German political philosopher and economist Karl Marx,* who argued that the conflict inherent in economic systems was the major force behind historical change. They agreed that culture could not be studied separately from social structures and power relationships.

Appadurai added that inequality and power are complicated by disjunctures* in global cultural flows and the work of the social imagination.* (Disjunctures occur when two different flows create conflicting conditions.) Appadurai writes, "[E]ven the meanest and most hopeless of lives, the most brutal and dehumanizing of circumstances, the harshest of lived inequalities are now open to the play of the imagination."[1] In other words, even if people suffer because of globalization,* they still have agency* (the capacity to make decisions and act, in their particular circumstances) in the form of choosing how to imagine new worlds and new lives for themselves.

The political scientist and historian Benedict Anderson also explored the political role of imagination. Anderson argued that the production and circulation of newspapers and books—"print-capitalism"*—helped to create a sense of nationalism* (an ideology expressing the strong belief that the identity or interests of an ethnic group or nation-state are of primary importance), resulting in an "imagined community"* (a group of people who feel that they have an important part of their identity in common with each other, even if they have never met).

Appadurai argues that globalization has sped up and intensified the process that Anderson described. Now the imagined community can stretch across national or regional borders.

Academic Influences

Scholars in many different disciplines recognized the importance of power and domination in understanding culture. This led them to the theory that cultural imperialism* leads to a homogenization* of cultures around the world. Local cultures would eventually be wiped out, and different populations across the world would become more and more culturally similar. Appadurai argued instead that globalization was leading to the heterogenization* of culture, creating new and hybrid cultural forms.

Appadurai was deeply involved in conversations about globalization and transnationalism (a theoretical perspective emphasizing global connections) during the period when he wrote *Modernity at Large*. He developed the idea for the book while a MacArthur Fellow* at the Institute for Advanced Study in Princeton and wrote it while codirector of the Center for Transnational* Cultural Studies at the University of Pennsylvania. The book was finished during his time at the University of Chicago, where he developed and served as director of the Globalization Project (a group of people working in different academic disciplines studying the economic, political, and cultural links between different countries).

Among anthropologists, Appadurai is known for advancing the importance of the study of global dimensions of culture. This ability to bridge the gap between the fields of globalization studies and anthropology is one of Appadurai's unique contributions.

---

1. Arjun Appadurai, *Modernity at Large: Cultural Dimensions of Globalization* (Minneapolis: University of Minnesota Press, 1996), 54.

MODULE 3
THE PROBLEM

KEY POINTS

* Appadurai argues for the study of globalization's* cultural dimensions through the idea of global cultural flows.* He points to the importance of electronic media* and migration,* which circulate ideas and people around the world.

* Before the publication of *Modernity at Large*, academics trying to theorize globalization tended to focus on inequality and how it is leading to the homogenization* of culture—societies all over the world becoming more similar to each other—or else they did not address the cultural dimensions of globalization at all.

* Appadurai argues that globalization is leading to a heterogenization* of culture—societies all over the world becoming more different from each other—that requires new theories and methods for studying the modern world.

Core Question

In the 1990s, when Arjun Appadurai began writing the essays included in *Modernity at Large: Cultural Dimensions of Globalization*, he was part of the growing field of globalization studies. While many theorists of globalization focused primarily on its political and economic dimensions, Appadurai argued for the importance of its cultural dimensions.

In Appadurai's primary field of anthropology,* some scholars were beginning to think about how globalization was affecting local culture. Previously, American anthropologists had focused on studying small-scale, relatively isolated societies through the lens of holism, a perspective on culture that emphasizes how cultural beliefs and practices function as a whole system.

Appadurai and other anthropology scholars argued against this. They were in favor of new methods and theories that would acknowledge that even seemingly isolated locations are caught up in global cultural flows. Rather than holism, Appadurai and others emphasized rupture*—how cultural practices split off from their origins.

Increasing numbers of people leave the country of their birth to live somewhere else, traveling and absorbing cultural influences from many places. A modern anthropology must reflect that international cultural flows are now more intense and work in new ways.

> *"The central problem of today's global interactions is the tension between cultural homogenization and cultural heterogenization."*
>
> —— Arjun Appadurai, *Modernity at Large: Cultural Dimensions of Globalization*

The Participants

Appadurai was in conversation with other scholars of globalization who were seeking to answer similar questions about processes of heterogenization and homogenization, power, and inequality. They wanted to create new theories and methods that could capture the processes of deterritorialization* and global cultural flows.

Outside of anthropology, many scholars were concerned that globalization would lead to homogenization, primarily through cultural imperialism.* For example John Tomlinson,* professor of English, culture, and media at Nottingham Trent University, described globalization as "the installation worldwide of Western versions of basic sociocultural reality: the West's ... theories, its values, ethical systems, approaches to rationality, technical-scientific world view, political culture, and so on."[1] The West dominates the world through cultural imperialism, spreading not only Western food, fashion, and language, but also Western world views and values.

Anthropologists generally agreed with Appadurai's thesis of heterogenization and criticized scholars like Tomlinson for painting a picture of non-Westerners as passive consumers of Western products and ideas. The most prominent of these anthropologists was Ulf Hannerz,* currently emeritus professor of anthropology at the University of Stockholm in Sweden. Hannerz's work was similar to Appadurai's theories of the transnational* interconnectedness of peoples around the world, a condition that Hannerz called the "global ecumene."*[2] This term refers to the idea that different societies, economies, and cultures make up one interconnected world.

Hannerz went even further than Appadurai in claiming that people affected by globalization are still able to gain agency,* or free choice, within their circumstances. He described how people living in non-Western societies are "speaking back" to globalization through the process of what he calls creolization:* the mixing of multiple cultural forms.[3]

The Contemporary Debate

Appadurai argued that heterogenization of culture is what makes our era one of modernity.* With people and ideas circulating the world, individuals and groups can imagine new identities and lives. They can construct these imagined lives around mixtures of cultural forms, practices, and ideas. Appadurai provides several examples, such as the sport of cricket. The British took cricket to India during the colonial* era (that is, at the height of British political dominance and exploitation), and high-status Indians began to play it in the late nineteenth century. At that time, the sport expressed the values of upper-class British masculinity. It is now played by people in the former British colonies and other countries, includes players from diverse ethnic and religious groups, and involves multiple levels of media expression.The global popularity of cricket is a clear example of heterogenization and of the deep historical perspective required to understand it.

The debate on culture and globalization continues today. Other scholars, including Hannerz, have written about migration, media, and other cultural flows. But Appadurai's big concepts, neologisms (that is, newly invented terms, such as "ethnoscapes") and convincing writing style have ensured that he continues to be the major academic voice representing the cultural dimensions of globalization.

1. John Tomlinson, "Internationalism, Globalization, and Cultural Imperialism," in *Media and Cultural Regulation*, ed. Kenneth Thompson (London: Sage Publications, 1997), 14.

2. Ulf Hannerz, *Cultural Complexity: Studies in the Social Organization of Meaning* (New York: Columbia University Press, 1992), 217.

3. Hannerz, *Cultural Complexity*, 256.

MODULE 4
THE AUTHOR'S CONTRIBUTION

KEY POINTS

* Appadurai's main aim in *Modernity at Large* is to provoke new theories and methods for understanding globalization* through the framework of global cultural flows.*

* Appadurai places an original emphasis on how migration* and electronic media* are producing new forms of social imagination.*

* The book built on previous theories of modernity* and imagination in order to show that the modern world is characterized by new and more intense interactions between people and ideas.

Author's Aims

Throughout *Modernity at Large: Cultural Dimensions of Globalization*, Arjun Appadurai's objective is to illustrate how migration and media influence societies in a world deterritorialized* (that is, where people and things become less tied to their places of origin) through the social imagination. Before this book, studies of globalization tended to focus on economics and politics as the causes of new global processes and structures. The global circulation of people and ideas was seen as an effect of globalization rather than a cause.

Appadurai focuses on two global cultural flows, migration and electronic media, insisting that they are an important part of globalization and a force for change. With the help of migration and electronic media, groups of people are together able to imagine new lives and worlds that were beyond the possibilities available earlier in history. Before modernity, the imagination was limited by the norms of an individual's or group's community or locale. Today, with access to people and ideas from around the world, people are able to see and imagine other ways of thinking and living.

> "[T]he world has been a congeries [a jumbled collection] of large-scale interactions for many centuries.Yet today's world involves interactions of a new order and intensity."
>
> —— Arjun Appadurai, *Modernity at Large: Cultural Dimensions of Globalization*

Approach

Modernity at Large inspired anthropologists and others to imagine new theories and methods for understanding culture. Although Appadurai draws upon past theories from disciplines including anthropology and area studies,* he criticizes their assumption that culture is a specific thing tied to a particular place. This supposition no longer applies to the way people live in the world, if it ever did.

Appadurai recreates the speed,intensity,and chaos of globalization through his writing style. He throws big ideas and concepts at the reader, and rushes through complicated examples to illustrate his points. In this way, he explains two global cultural flows of particular importance: migration and electronic media.

The book makes the case that migration and electronic media, along with the decline of the nation-state,* have resulted in new diasporic* publics (that is, group identities that exist across national and other spatial boundaries). In the third part of the book, Appadurai argues that these flows are crucial to modern movements based on shared ethnic identities, which he refers to as culturalisms.* Powered by the forces of migration and electronic media, culturalisms often lead to conflicts over cultural or national spaces. Appadurai's concept of the social imagination shows how global cultural flows can both create group identities and bring them into conflict.

Contribution in Context

Appadurai is uncomfortable with theories in Western social science that assume modernity is a universally desired state. He criticizes the way that this assumption appears in modernization theory,* the American sociological theory of the 1950s and 1960s influenced by the pioneering German sociologist Max Weber* and the Frankfurt School* (a school of social thought associated both with the Institute for Social Research at Goethe University in Frankfurt, Germany, and a critique of capitalism influenced by the thought of the German political philosopher Karl Marx). Modernization theory predicted that "the imagination will be stunted"[1] by capitalism, secularization, and other processes that helped to create our global world.

However, rather than stunting the imagination of the masses, "the consumption of the mass media throughout the world often provokes resistance, irony, selectivity, and, in general, *agency*."*[2] Individuals and communities do not simply consume electronic media passively, but use it to build their identities.

To make this point, Appadurai puts a new twist on the concept of the imagined community* discussed by political scientist and historian Benedict Anderson.* Anderson argued that the development of print-capitalism* (national media such as books and newspapers) allowed groups of people to develop a sense of shared identity. In particular, citizens of a nation-state developed a sense of nationalism, partly through reading newspapers and other print media in a shared language. Appadurai joins this concept to his own notion of a "community of sentiment," "a group that begins to imagine and feel things together."[3] This collective imagination, built through migration and mass media, allows people to build a shared sense of identity across national and other spatial boundaries.

Appadurai's argument is original because it focuses on "the everyday cultural practice through which the work of the imagination is transformed."[4] He wants to create a theoretical approach that reflects the fact that people do not simply accept and follow the rules and norms of their social context—they also work collectively to imagine new rules and norms.

---

1. Arjun Appadurai, *Modernity at Large: Cultural Dimensions of Globalization* (Minneapolis: University of Minnesota Press, 1996), 6.

2. Appadurai, *Modernity at Large*, 7.

3. Appadurai, *Modernity at Large*, 8.

4. Appadurai, *Modernity at Large*, 9.

SECTION 2
IDEAS

MAIN IDEAS

KEY POINTS

- Appadurai addresses three key themes throughout *Modernity at Large*: he describes five dimensions of global cultural flows;* he explores the impact of migration* and electronic media* on how people imagine themselves and their worlds; and he introduces a new framework for studying culture and globalization.*

- His main argument is that culture, rather than economics, should be central to analyses of globalization.

- Appadurai's arguments are broad and sweeping, but he provides several examples from colonial* and contemporary India to illustrate them.

Key Themes

In *Modernity at Large: Cultural Dimensions of Globalization*, Arjun Appadurai describes five global cultural flows, which he refers to as "scapes"*—mediascapes and financescapes, for example. Global cultural flows are a result of globalization, and influence individuals and communities. Gaps in the relationships between different flows result in disjunctures*—or points of disconnect—that Appadurai urges us to study in relation to globalization.

Two kinds of global flow are of particular interest to Appadurai: the circulation of people through migration, and the circulation of ideas through electronic media. These flows expose people to worlds beyond their original locality or nation-state.*

Today, people everywhere are able to imagine "a wider set of possible lives than they ever did before."[1]

Appadurai distinguishes between "culture" and "cultural." During most of the twentieth century, American anthropologists tended to focus on the local and the particular, approaching culture as "some kind of object, thing, or substance."[2] Appadurai prefers the word "cultural" to "culture," because it "moves one into a realm of differences, contrasts, and comparisons that is more helpful."[3] Culture is not a single, fixed thing; rather, we forge our sense of ourselves and the world from a multiplicity of material. Appadurai argues that anthropologists today must not rely on outdated concepts of identity, but should instead account for how people build identities in a modern globalized world. A person's identity does not emerge fully formed from their birthplace or heritage. It is created through comparison and contrast with the diverse communities with whom they come into contact through migration and electronic media.

> "There has been a general change in the global conditions of lifeworlds."
>
> —— Arjun Appadurai, *Modernity at Large: Cultural Dimensions of Globalization*

Exploring the Ideas

Appadurai begins the book by addressing the question of modernity:* a set of attitudes, technologies, and social forms generally associated with Western countries in the twentieth century, which also marks the time we are living in now. Appadurai argues for the existence of a variety of modernities. As people and ideas circulate around the globalized world, differences become apparent. These differences allow people to make comparisons and use their imaginations to understand their particular place in the globalized world.

The title *Modernity at Large* is meant to convey that modernity does not exist in a particular place but is "at large," experienced in different ways by different people living in a globalized world. These differences result in disjunctures when and where there are gaps or contradictions between different global flows. Appadurai gives an example of a disjuncture in Japan: the country's openness to new ideas and foreign products is at odds with the government's unwillingness to accept immigrants.

In order to analyze these disjunctures, Appadurai proposes an innovative framework for anthropologists and other social scientists. This framework categorizes global cultural flows into five dimensions:

- ethnoscapes*
- technoscapes*
- financescapes*
- mediascapes*
- ideoscapes*

The suffix "scapes" is meant to capture their fluidity within and beyond the borders of nation-states and the irregularity of their form.

Ethnoscapes comprise the "landscape of persons" whose

identity crosses, moves between, and influences national boundaries. So Appadurai's concept of ethnoscapes emphasizes immigrants, tourists, and other people on the move. Technoscapes and financescapes refer to the global patterns of technology and money: how they develop and move across boundaries. Mediascapes and ideoscapes are landscapes of images. Mediascapes present visual narratives through electronic media, providing substance for viewers' imagined selves and imagined worlds. Ideoscapes tend to be political representations that relate to national or state ideologies.

This five-part framework examines links and ruptures* among different global cultural flows. Deterritorialization* is a key part of the process, as people, ideas, and cultural forms are moved away from their original contexts and placed in new ones.

Language and Expression

Modernity at Large is a collection of nine essays reworked from previous publications, divided into three sections. The first three chapters introduce the main themes and arguments and describe Appadurai's framework for a "transnational* anthropology."[4] They argue against previous theories of modernity and for an emphasis on culture in studies of globalization.

The book is intended for those involved in the social sciences and particularly the study of globalization. The rapid flow of words and examples mimics the rapid flow of ideas and people that are described in the text.

Appadurai coins new terms such as "post-blurring" (the

modern condition in which already blurred boundaries get even more blurred by globalization) and "gray markets" (economic flows between formal, or white, markets and informal, or black, markets). Some of his new terms have become standard in anthropology, including "scapes" and "disjunctures." He assumes the reader is already familiar with key concepts from the social sciences, and while he provides summaries within each section and a conclusion at the end of each chapter, his arguments are often so broad and sweeping that they are difficult to grasp in detail.

The second set of three chapters illustrates Appadurai's points through examples related to British colonialism,* involving consumption and fashion, sport, and census-taking. The final three chapters turn toward the future, particularly that of the nation-state model in a world of postnational* identities and locations (that is, a world in which the nation-state as an entity no longer exists or is much weaker than before).

---

1. Arjun Appadurai, *Modernity at Large: Cultural Dimensions of Globalization* (Minneapolis: University of Minnesota Press, 1996), 53.

2. Appadurai, *Modernity at Large*, 12.

3. Appadurai, *Modernity at Large*, 12.

4. Appadurai, *Modernity at Large*, 48.

MODULE 6
SECONDARY IDEAS

KEY POINTS

* An important secondary idea in *Modernity at Large* is that the nation-state* is in crisis and that the world is becoming postnational* (i.e. nations no longer matter in a globalized world).

* Relatedly, culturalism* is often linked to ethnic violence (violence between groups whose racial or ethnic identities give them different access to power or resources).

* Although ethnic violence is the main topic of a whole chapter and other portions of the book, Appadurai's ideas on ethnic violence were overshadowed by his arguments related to modernity* and globalization.*

Other Ideas

An important secondary idea in Arjun Appadurai's *Modernity at Large: Cultural Dimensions of Globalization* is that the nation-state is in crisis. He argues that this crisis is best understood through its cultural dimensions. Because people share identities that stretch across the borders of nation-states, they may no longer primarily identify with one particular nationality.

Culturalism is a related form of identity-building taking place at the level of the nation-state. Nations are composed of people with different ethnic identities, but governments promote the idea of the nation as made up of fixed categories of people. Members of those categories have worked within them in order to access entitlements (government programs that provide benefits to a particular group) or find safety in numbers.

Sometimes this can become transnational,* as groups choose to mobilize around shared aspects of their identities with similar groups in other nation-states. For example, many indigenous groups throughout the world connect with each other through a shared experience of being marginalized within their respective nation-states.

Appadurai links culturalism to the problem of ethnic violence. However, his insightful discussions of ethnic violence in *Modernity at Large* were eclipsed by his core arguments about modernity and global cultural flows.* He extended and further developed them in later works, most notably in *Fear of Small Numbers: An Essay on the Geography of Anger.*[1]

> *"I have come to be convinced that the nation-state, as a complex modern political form, is on its last legs."*
>
> —— Arjun Appadurai, *Modernity at Large: Cultural Dimensions of Globalization*

Exploring the Ideas

According to Appadurai, nation-states "make sense only as parts of a system."[2] The actions of nation-states no longer determine the course of history. Scholars in other fields, particularly comparative politics* (an academic methodology that compares the politics, institutions, and conflicts of different countries or eras) have also acknowledged that the nation-state is in crisis.

Because people's shared identities stretch across the borders of nation-states, they may no longer primarily identify with one particular state. Other systems and relationships (such as interlinked diaspora* identities, forms of religious fundamentalism, or ethnic nationalisms*) are becoming more important than nation-states in building individual and group identities.

Appadurai defines culturalism as "identity politics mobilized at the level of the nation-state."[3] ("Identity politics" refers to political views and political action based on a particular ethnic, class, gender, or other form of identity.) He defines the term "culturalism" through a long discussion of his distinction between the terms "culture"* and "cultural." Culture has too often been understood by anthropologists* "as an object or thing that groups of people possess."[4] By contrast, the word "cultural" stresses the dimensionality or multiplicity of culture, as a device that allows anthropologists to think about difference.[5] Culture is not a fixed thing but a dimension of identity that only becomes clear through difference or contrast.

Culturalism is the use of group identities for political purposes, often in order to challenge the nation-state. Culturalist movements are "the most general form of the work of the imagination and draw frequently on the fact or possibility of migration* or secession [regions or groups becoming independent from a bigger political entity]."[6] Appadurai argues that culturalism is the primary form that cultural differences tend to take today and represents a major challenge to the stability of the nation-state.

Overlooked

Appadurai argues against more prevalent theories of ethnic identity as natural or primordial* (a characterization of ethnic identity based on strong attachments to a shared biological essence or kinship), instead showing that ethnicity is constructed as a localized response to global cultural forces.

A group is not necessarily born with an ethnic identity. Rather, a group mobilizes an ethnic identity based on cultural aspects such as language, religion, and food. Sometimes such mobilization takes place on a large scale, across nation-state boundaries, or sometimes a group may claim that its identity is based on a particular locale.

Ethnic violence is particularly bloody within the modern nation-state system. Appadurai writes: "The worst kinds of violence in these wars appear to have something to do with the distorted relationship between daily, face-to-face relations and the large-scale identities produced by modern nation-states and complicated by large-scale diasporas."[7] Appadurai's argument about ethnic violence adds nuance to his larger argument about global identity-making and the use of the social imagination.* The social imagination may be at work on a global scale, allowing people to imagine new worlds and new lives, but ethnic violence can result when very localized identities are mobilized across spatial boundaries and come into conflict with the nation-state.

1. Arjun Appadurai, *Fear of Small Numbers: An Essay on the Geography of Anger* (Durham, NC: Duke University Press, 2006).
2. Arjun Appadurai, *Modernity at Large: Cultural Dimensions of Globalization* (Minneapolis: University of Minnesota Press, 1996), 19.
3. Appadurai, *Modernity at Large*, 15.
4. Appadurai, *Modernity at Large*, 12.
5. Appadurai, *Modernity at Large*, 12.
6. Appadurai, *Modernity at Large*, 15.
7. Appadurai, *Modernity at Large*, 154.

ACHIEVEMENT

KEY POINTS

* Appadurai's groundbreaking *Modernity at Large* added a fresh perspective to studies of culture in a globalized* world.

* The book builds on his earlier seminal essay "Disjuncture* and Difference in the Global Cultural Economy," and provides examples to support his points about the role of migration* and electronic media* in the social imagination.*

* Appadurai suggests areas for ethnographic* research but does not contribute empirical* data from any research of his own.

Assessing the Argument

In *Modernity at Large: Cultural Dimensions of Globalization*, Arjun Appadurai describes how global cultural flows,* especially migration and electronic media, are allowing people to imagine their world and lives in new ways. He then shows how these new forms can be used to explain ethnic violence and social movements today. The essay was an expansion of ideas presented in his earlier "Disjuncture and Difference in the Global Cultural Economy," published in 1990 in the journal *Theory, Culture, and Society*.[1] This essay is chapter 2 in *Modernity at Large*.

One of the enduring contributions of the original article and the book as a whole is their elaboration of the concept of "scapes"*—of people, finance, technologies, images, and ideas. A group of sociologists in Great Britain, among them Martin Albrow,* have worked to extend the notion of "scapes" into new areas of research. Albrow writes that the term "'scapes' unlocks a perspective for empirical social research that can do more justice to local/global relations than older notions of community and neighborhood."[2]

> "As a stimulus to the sociological imagination for current research, Appadurai has few rivals."
>
> —— Martin Albrow, "Review of *Modernity at Large*,"
> *American Journal of Sociology*

Achievement in Context

Appadurai's "Disjuncture and Difference in the Global Cultural Economy" was one in a series of essays about cultural dimensions of globalization.* Scholars in several fields were attempting to make sense of the ways that globalization had subsequently led to an unlinking of place and people, cultural practices, and ideas, around the world. At the same time, anthropologists were debating whether this deterritorialization* was actually new or simply a more rapid form of the same processes of cultural contact and change that had always characterized human existence.

The field of globalization studies was still largely focused on political and economic factors and often saw cultural change as a secondary effect of globalization rather than a primary component. Through *Modernity at Large*, Appadurai attempted to outline a research agenda for studying culture in a globalized world. One of his major, but most controversial, contributions was his observation that there are new forms of social imagination in the world today, produced by global cultural flows and producing, in their own turn, new forms of identity across nation-state* and other spatial boundaries. Imagination is an elusive concept and difficult to research empirically. The ability of an individual or group of people to imagine new worlds and new lives is a sign that they have agency*—that is, the ability to act and make choices within the limits of their circumstances.

While this idea was appealing to scholars of culture within globalization studies, it was unappealing to those whose theories emphasized the political and economic structures of globalization.

Limitations

The major limitation of *Modernity at Large* is its lack of foundation in empirical evidence. Appadurai's examples are based on his observations and readings, rather than on methodologically sound research.

At the time of the book's publication (1996), many anthropologists were increasingly critical of how globalization was worsening inequality between people and states. Appadurai's emphasis on agency through the social imagination is sometimes viewed as disguising the constraints on the life choices of individuals and groups.

---

1. Arjun Appadurai, "Disjuncture and Difference in the Global Cultural Economy," *Theory, Culture, and Society* 7, no. 2 (June 1990): 295–310.
2. Martin Albrow, "Review: *Modernity at Large: Cultural Dimensions of Globalization* by Arjun Appadurai," *American Journal of Sociology* 103, no.5 (March 1998), 1412.

MODULE 8
PLACE IN THE AUTHOR'S WORK

KEY POINTS

* Appadurai's chief focus throughout his life's work has been to provide and inspire new ways of understanding cultural dimensions of globalization.*

* Appadurai has published 13 books, and *Modernity at Large* is among his best-known works.

* Since the publication of *Modernity at Large* in 1996, Appadurai has continued to elaborate and illustrate the concepts and methods introduced in the book.

Positioning

Arjun Appadurai's *Modernity at Large: Cultural Dimensions of Globalization* is a collection of essays that he wrote over six years. The book brings together many recurring themes from his earlier academic career, such as consumption, colonization,* and migration.* Most of the chapters are revised versions of earlier published work. The book clarifies ideas about how culture flows through the global economy and offers direction for future studies of globalization.

Following *Modernity at Large*, Appadurai published two works that extended his important contributions to globalization studies. He contributed a chapter, "Grassroots Globalization and the Research Imagination,"[1] to *Globalization* (2001),[2] a volume he himself edited. The essay is an important commentary on the relationship between research and globalization.

The second work, *Fear of Small Numbers: An Essay on the Geography of Anger* (2006),[3] can be considered a response to the criticism that his earlier works did not adequately address the negative side of globalization. The text focuses on the relationship of ethnic violence to globalization, an elaboration on themes introduced in one chapter of *Modernity at Large*.

His most recent book, *The Future as a Cultural Fact: Essays on the Global Condition* (2013),[4] is described as a sequel to *Modernity at Large* and attempts to lay out more clearly a research agenda for future studies of the cultural dimensions of globalization. The text addresses similar themes to those seen in *Modernity at Large*, this time drawing on firsthand research in Mumbai slums.

> "Modernity at Large *remains testimony to the theoretical and methodological contributions that transnational* anthropology and historiography have to offer in an era of globalization and ethnic violence.*"
>
> —— D. A. De Zoysa, "Review of *Modernity at Large*,"
> *International Migration Review*

Integration

Early in Appadurai's life, as a student in the United States, he was wary of theories that made modernity* sound like a universal goal or that associated modernity with certain places. As he continued his studies in anthropology and area studies,* he grew critical of the tendency in these fields to locate culture in a single place or region. Many of his perspectives came about through his experiences as an

Indian who had moved to the United States.

Appadurai's work addresses these early observations and concerns. He attempts to define modernity as a fragmented* set of different perspectives. He recognizes that new theories and methods are required to account for cultural change and human agency* within globalization. Using his grounding in theories of capitalism formulated by Karl Marx,* he updates Marx for a global world of complicated identities. He also shows how better studies of globalization can help explain such diverse phenomena as ethnic violence and patterns of media consumption.

Over time, Appadurai has attempted to clarify concepts and suggestions for research made in his earlier works. His recent publications have also answered the criticisms that his big ideas are not sufficiently grounded in empirical* research. He has drawn more and more on his Indian background and used examples from India to illustrate his arguments.

Significance

Appadurai's work has been highly influential. Although he has now published 13 books and over 90 articles, *Modernity at Large* remains his most important work.

When *Modernity at Large* was published in 1996, the field of globalization studies was relatively new, as were studies in anthropology that took seriously global aspects of culture. Appadurai's early interventions in those fields have ensured that *Modernity at Large* will be a classic of late twentieth-century anthropology. Although Appadurai's later works have been well received and introduced new concepts and methods in their own right, he will be primarily associated with the theories of "scapes"* (the term he coined to indicate the distribution and movement of things, ideas, and images around the world, used as a suffix in words like mediascape and technoscape), disjuncture* (a point of disconnect or separation), and social imagination*—concepts that were introduced in *Modernity at Large*.

1. Arjun Appadurai, "Grassroots Globalization and the Research Imagination," in *Globalization*, ed. Arjun Appadurai (Durham, NC: Duke University Press, 2001), 1–21.

2. Arjun Appadurai, ed., *Globalization* (Durham, NC: Duke University Press, 2001).

3. Arjun Appadurai, *Fear of Small Numbers: An Essay on the Geography of Anger* (Durham, NC: Duke University Press, 2006).

4. Arjun Appadurai, *The Future as Cultural Fact: Essays on the Global Condition* (New York: Verso, 2013).

SECTION 3
IMPACT

MODULE 9
THE FIRST RESPONSES

KEY POINTS

* There are three major critiques of Arjun Appadurai's *Modernity at Large*: that it is not based on empirical* research; that it overstates the agency* of individuals and groups; and that it presents a vision of globalization* that is too optimistic.

* In later works Appadurai wrote more about the negative side of globalization but continued to emphasize the agency of individuals and groups in building social movements to address it.

* Although Appadurai intended to reach a wide audience of people interested in globalization, those who have read and debated *Modernity at Large* mostly work in the disciplines of anthropology* and area studies.*

Criticism

For many cultural anthropologists, Arjun Appadurai's *Modernity at Large: Cultural Dimensions of Globalization* is not sufficiently based on ethnographic* fieldwork. As E. Paul Durrenberger,* emeritus professor of anthropology at Pennsylvania State University, writes: "Appadurai seems to have lost contact with the hard edges of ethnography and lived-in locales."[1]

Appadurai is often reluctant to state causality (the relationship between a cause and an effect). For example, he writes that the British colonial* power in India used a census to count people and assign them to categories of caste (hereditary social class) and

116

religious affiliation. Over time, these categories became important components of group identity. These group identities have come into conflict, which has resulted in violence. Yet Appadurai is unclear whether practices that count and categorize people such as the census *caused, shaped,* or simply *established some conditions for* contemporary ethnic violence among South Asians. Appadurai cannot clarify his position because of a lack of empirical evidence. Thus, the "rhetoric of this piece is one of persuasion by forcefully stated opinion rather than appeal to evidence."[2]

A second objection to the book is that Appadurai is not sufficiently critical of globalization. For those who see globalization as a system that structurally relies on inequality, Appadurai's ideas about the social imagination* paint an unrealistic picture of a world in which all people and groups are free to imagine the world and their lives in their own way. His insistence on heterogenization*—a process in which cultural aspects combine and change to become more diverse—ignores the ways that government, finance, and labor impose their own order and limit the choices that individuals and communities are able to make.

Modernity at Large has not been cited widely by scholars in political science and economics. One scholar notes that "his appealing rhetoric made him very popular among postmodernists."[3] Postmodernist* scholars argue that the meanings of representations and interpretations depend on perspective rather than fixed truths. This approach has remained popular in disciplines such as literary criticism and anthropology but has held little appeal in political science and economics.

Responses

Appadurai's work discusses globalization as a crucial feature of the modern world, characterized by global cultural flows.* His goal is to improve the study of globalization through better theories and methods that acknowledge the present conditions of the world, rather than to prescribe changes. For that reason, he seems uninterested in characterizing globalization as either "good" or "bad."

He describes how globalization enables social movements to fight back against its own negative forces. In this way, globalization makes for "a level playing field" in the sense that "when there are solutions to the problem of everyday life, they can be made available to a wider population than was originally possible, and more quickly through the Internet, through other kinds of media, through word of mouth; through travel and through all the methods available through technology."4 Globalization speeds up and spreads solutions as well as problems.

Appadurai says that his lack of interest in causality is intentional. He writes that "one cannot come to a given situation with a strong prior sense about how the causal flows work. That form is what the word 'disjuncture'* captures."[5] The contradictions and gaps between different flows mean that any situation will turn out to be made up of a unique and unexpected combination of causes and effects.

Conflict and Consensus

Appadurai uses his own general observations and experiences rather than empirical research to illustrate his points. For example, he analyzes how Indians transformed cricket from a sport associated with elite Victorian-era British masculinity into one associated with fragmented,* contemporary, Indian masculinities. The absence of empirical evidence in *Modernity at Large* seems deliberate. Several times in the book he points out that a particular argument or example needs to be followed up with appropriate research.

In later works, Appadurai directly addressed the debate about whether or not he presents a too-positive view of globalization. In his book *Fear of Small Numbers* (2006), he writes, "Some critics saw [*Modernity at Large*] as presenting too rosy a picture of the globalization of the early 1990s and as being insufficiently attentive to the darker sides of globalization, such as violence, exclusion, and growing inequality. In part as a consequence of these questions, and in part driven by my own longer-term interests, I began to do research on collective violence against Muslims in my home city."[6] This research shows that globalization produces violence as well as agency.*

1. E. Paul Durrenberger, "Review: Anthropology and Globalization," *American Anthropologist* 103, no. 1 (June 2001), 533.

2. Durrenberger, "Review," 534.

3. Gijsbert Oonk, "Review: *Modernity at Large: Cultural Dimensions of Globalization* by Arjun Appadurai," *Journal of World History* 11, no. 1 (Spring 2000), 158.

4. John C. Hawley, "Postscript: An Interview with Arjun Appadurai," in *The Postcolonial and the Global*, ed. Revathi Krishnaswamy and John C. Hawley (Minneapolis: University of Minnesota Press, 2007), 293.

5. Arjun Appadurai, "Illusion of Permanence: Interview with Arjun Appadurai," *Perspecta* 34 (2003), 45.

6. Arjun Appadurai, *Fear of Small Numbers: An Essay on the Geography of Anger* (Durham NC: Duke University Press, 2006), ix–x.

MODULE 10
THE EVOLVING DEBATE

KEY POINTS

- Appadurai's concept of "scapes"* as sites of disjuncture* provided a framework for anthropologists* studying culture in a globalized world.

- Appadurai's ideas on global cultural flows* have been used by most scholars of cultural dimensions of globalization* writing in the last two decades.

- While Appadurai's work has been used in a variety of fields, from sociology to urban planning, his core followers can be found among anthropologists and other social scientists seeking to understand culture and globalization.

Uses and Problems

Arjun Appadurai's theory of global cultural flows, as set out in *Modernity at Large: Cultural Dimensions of Globalization,* offers a productive starting point for studying what is distinctly modern about globalization. Many people now share his view that what is characteristically modern about globalization is reflected in the unpredictable movements of ideas, things, and people that he terms "cultural flows."

The majority of references to the text relate to Appadurai's theory that there are five "scapes" of global cultural flows: ethnoscapes,* technoscapes,* financescapes,* mediascapes,* and ideoscapes.* Others have built on Appadurai's work by naming other important "scapes," or examining how these five "scapes" appear in particular locations.

Appadurai's emphasis on the social imagination* was favorably received as a contribution to a longer-term attempt to understand human agency* within global cultural forces. His approach to the imagination draws on a long tradition, dating back to the pioneering sociologists Emile Durkheim* and Max Weber,* and traveling through the scholar of nationalism* Benedict Anderson* by way of the influential French sociologist and anthropologist Pierre Bourdieu,* so Appadurai's theory of the imagination has not contributed to his reputation and fame as much as his newly coined word "scapes."

> *"[One] seldom comes across a graduate student nowadays whose project does not bear in some way or another on global disjunctures … In this context, Appadurai's article marks a watershed."*
>
> ——Peter Metcalf, "Global 'Disjuncture' and the 'Sites' of Anthropology," *Cultural Anthropology*

Schools of Thought

Modernity at Large remains an important book within globalization studies and has been cited almost 20,000 times, according to Google Scholar. Many writers, academics, and thinkers have been influenced by it.

The breadth and vagueness of the ideas presented in the book do not seem intended to start a new academic tradition but, rather, to inspire others to include new elements in existing ways of studying culture and cultural contact. *Modernity at Large* is part of "a long-term project—both intellectual and personal—to seek ways to make globalization work for those who need it most and enjoy it least, the poor, the dispossessed, the weak, and the marginal populations of our world."[1] For example, after later research in the slums of the Indian city of Mumbai, Appadurai wrote about the ways urban planning can respond to the imagination and expectations of impoverished slum-dwellers.

In Current Scholarship

In the two decades since *Modernity at Large* was published, its ideas and challenges have been taken up by most scholars trying to understand culture in today's globalized world or explain social change in particular communities and locales.

Some have built on Appadurai's work by naming other important "scapes" in addition to the five he outlined. For example, Martin Albrow* and other sociologists in the United Kingdom have developed the concept of "socioscapes,"* or flows of relationships and networks. Albrow writes: "We think 'scapes' unlocks a perspective for empirical* social research that can do more justice to local/global relations than older notions of community and neighborhood."[2]

Other scholars have examined how the five "scapes" are present in particular places. Peter Metcalf,* professor emeritus of anthropology at the University of Virginia, and other anthropologists have found that the concept of "scapes" provides a good basis for understanding the profound and rapid change faced in the last few decades by the populations they study. Metcalf writes of his own ethnographic studies in Borneo that "applying Appadurai's model brought home to me clearly the way in which the upriver world that I knew in the Seventies has been pulled apart by social forces of enormous reach and power, acting not in concert, nor even in competition, but in a kind of mindless cupidity."[3]

---

1. Arjun Appadurai, *Fear of Small Numbers: An Essay on the Geography of Anger* (Durham NC: Duke University Press, 2006), xi.

2. Martin Albrow, "Review: *Modernity at Large: Cultural Dimensions of Globalization* by Arjun Appadurai," *American Journal of Sociology* 103, no.5 (March 1998): 1412.

3. Peter Metcalf, "Global 'Disjuncture' and the 'Sites' of Anthropology," *Cultural Anthropology* 16, no. 2: 173.

MODULE 11
IMPACT AND INFLUENCE TODAY

KEY POINTS

- Published 20 years ago, *Modernity at Large* is quickly becoming a classic in the anthropology* of globalization.*

- Appadurai argued that globalization studies must take into account cultural, as well as economic and political, dimensions of globalization.

- The challenges presented in *Modernity at Large* have for the most part been ignored by economists.

Position

Arjun Appadurai's *Modernity at Large: Cultural Dimensions of Globalization* was published as part of a conversation with others working in the same field, when globalization studies was still a new academic discipline. The subtitle of the book indicates its intention to address the cultural extent of globalization.

Appadurai challenged anthropologists to rethink their methods of studying culture by acknowledging the deterritorialization* of people and cultural practices brought about by globalization. He provided a framework based on five "scapes" of global cultural flows* (ethnoscapes,* technoscapes,* financescapes,* mediascapes,* and ideoscapes*) and the disjunctures*—the points of separation—between them.

For anthropologists, the text is set to become a classic, particularly its second chapter, "Disjuncture and Difference in the Global Cultural Economy." The book is cited in most works on the global elements of culture published by anthropologists in the last two decades.

Although the text has been useful to many disciplines, its major argument for the importance of cultural dimensions of globalization has, by and large, not convinced political scientists and, in particular, economists. Economists generally study globalization from a rational, top-down perspective that is interested in culture only when it offers possible explanations for individual and group consumer habits.

> "[A]nthropologists have essentially handed over the entire business of the future to economics."
>
> ——Arjun Appadurai, "Illusion of Permanence: Interview with Arjun Appadurai," *Perspecta*

Interaction

For Appadurai, acknowledging the importance of culture is crucial to economic analyses of globalization for at least three reasons.

First, while economic analyses present globalization as a smooth process, cultural analyses call attention to instability, diversity, and difference.

Second, economic analyses often predict homogenization,* arguing that the world is becoming smaller and more similar through globalization. Cultural analyses, by contrast, can emphasize heterogenization*—as people and ideas circulate around the world and stimulate the social imagination, they produce new or hybrid cultural forms.

Third, economic analyses lack a historical perspective, being too focused on individual activity, which does not sufficiently account for individuals as members of groups and communities with deep histories of nation, place, and identity. Cultural analyses can help people studying the contemporary globalized world to "look back" and see the roots of the present moment.

Appadurai does not necessarily blame economists for ignoring culture; he is more focused on encouraging anthropologists to insert cultural matters into economic analyses.

The Continuing Debate

Several scholars have addressed whether or not economic and cultural perspectives on a subject can be reconciled. For example, the University of California at Berkeley economists Pranab Bardhan* and Isha Ray* note that economics and anthropology "are often seen as extremes along the social science continuum"[1] because of their different theoretical and methodological concerns. One of the key differences is autonomy (economics) as opposed to embeddedness (anthropology). That is: economic analyses tend to view individuals as relatively autonomous agents choosing from the possibilities available to them, whereas anthropologists tend to view individuals as embedded in culture, making choices that can only be assessed in the context of their society.

A second key difference is between outcome (economics) and process (anthropology). While economists are looking for the outcomes of global structures, policies, and events, anthropologists are interested in the complex relationships and events through which outcomes develop. Similarly, a third difference lies between parsimony* (economics favors simple, linear explanations for the phenomena it studies) and complexity (anthropology aims to describe the intricacy of social worlds).

Economics and anthropology ask and answer very different kinds of questions about globalization. Although many respected anthropologists such as Arjun Appadurai, Clifford Geertz,* and Mary Douglas* have sought to undertake research with economists, the differences between the two disciplines have so far made attempts at combining them unsuccessful.

However, some economists have commented that economic projects suffer from a lack of cultural analysis. Amartya Sen,* an economics professor at Harvard University, concludes that "the cultural dimension of development requires closer scrutiny in development analysis."[2] Culture helps explain the political processes that underlie development projects or prevent them from being successful.

---

1. Pranab Bardhan and Isha Ray, "Methodological Approaches in Economics and Anthropology," *Q Squared Working Paper* 17 (Centre for International Studies, University of Toronto, February 2006), 1.

2. Amartya Sen, "How Does Culture Matter?" in *Culture and Public Action*, ed. Viyayendra Rao and Michael Walton (Stanford: Stanford University Press, 2004), 37.

MODULE 12
WHERE NEXT?

KEY POINTS

* Arjun Appadurai's work will continue to inspire anthropologists*
  and other social scientists.

* The book's emphasis on the cultural dimensions of
  globalization* may take on more resonance with economists
  and political scientists if anti-globalization social movements
  become more prominent and powerful.

* *Modernity at Large* is one of the most heavily cited works in the
  anthropology of globalization, particularly its second chapter,
  "Disjuncture and Difference in the Global Cultural Economy."

Potential

Arjun Appadurai's *Modernity at Large: Cultural Dimensions of Globalization* introduces important ideas about how anthropologists and others should conduct research in the context of globalization. Appadurai also introduces significant methodological insights that have proved to be helpful within globalization studies.

Although some critics have argued that Appadurai raises more questions than he answers, this can be seen as a strength of the book that will ensure its continued significance. Appadurai offers specific recommendations to readers on how they can use his ideas in their own research.

Modernity at Large is destined to become a classic in anthropology, representing a decisive moment in the discipline in the late twentieth century, when anthropologists were struggling to include modernity* and globalization in their studies of culture. Appadurai's emphasis on the heterogenization* of cultural forms helped anthropologists to link the global and the local.

Modernity at Large and other, later works by Appadurai have shaped debates about how globalization provokes and intensifies ethnic violence today.

> "[T]he task of ethnography now becomes the unraveling of a conundrum: what is the nature of locality as a lived experience in a globalized, deterritorialized world?"
>
> —— Arjun Appadurai, *Modernity at Large: Cultural Dimensions of Globalization*

Future Directions

Some social scientists are building on Appadurai's idea of "scapes." They are defining additional "scapes" where conjunctures* and disjunctures* occur among global cultural flows.* A group of sociologists working with the British scholar Martin Albrow* has theorized that socioscapes* are a sixth dimension of global cultural flows.[1] Socioscapes organize the relationships and networks of individuals within a community or locale.

Even Appadurai's critics still use the terms he invented, naming other "scapes" to show the limits of his theory. For example, the Dutch world historian Gijsbert Oonk* suggests that Appadurai could have included additional "scapes" related to science and the environment.[2] This criticism shows that, even among people who disagree with aspects of *Modernity at Large*, the book has the potential to forge new directions in research.

Appadurai hoped to inspire researchers in disciplines such as political science and economics to consider the cultural dimensions of globalization, but generally this audience has not been persuaded that culture is important in their analysis. However, as Appadurai predicted, transnational* social movements are growing, addressing human rights, women's rights, social justice for the poor, and other global issues. As these movements continue to grow, more scholars of globalization may well be persuaded that culture is important.

Summary

In *Modernity at Large*, Appadurai argues that scholars should study the cultural dimensions of globalization through the conjunctures and disjunctures between five "scapes," or dimensions of global cultural flows: ethnoscapes* (people), technoscapes* (technology), financescapes* (money), mediascapes* (images), and ideoscapes* (ideologies). He focuses on mass migration and electronic media as two important processes that move people and ideas around the world. These processes produce disjunctures where identities, ideas, and perspectives collide.

Though not based on Appadurai's own empirical* research, the work contains numerous ideas about how others can research "scapes" in a world that is increasingly deterritorialized* and transnational. For anthropologists, Appadurai suggests that cultural studies* provides useful methods for helping ethnographic* research reflect how human lives and ideas are connected across space and time through globalization.

Modernity at Large was published at a time when most academic thinking about globalization focused only on the ways it took power away from people. Appadurai's new ideas about globalization suggest that the picture is more complex, since humans also have agency* within the structures and processes of globalization. As people and ideas circulate and collide, the social imagination* enables people to picture new worlds and new lives for themselves. This act of the imagination, which draws upon a variety of factors, such as nostalgic memories of homeland, mass media, and life experiences, is an important driver of both positive and negative aspects of globalization.

These big ideas will continue to be used to address the questions posed by social scientists about people, culture, and the world system in an age when globalization has, ironically, both reinforced and removed the barriers between people and ideas.

---

1. Albrow, Martin, *The Global Age: State and Society beyond Modernity* (Stanford, CA: Stanford University Press, 1996).

2. Gijsbert Oonk, "Review: *Modernity at Large: Cultural Dimensions of Globalization* by Arjun Appadurai," *Journal of World History* 11, no. 1 (Spring 2000), 158.

GLOSSARY OF TERMS

1. **Agency:** the capacity of humans to act and make choices within their particular life conditions.

2. **Anthropology:** the systematic study of human behavior and practices.

3. **Area studies:** the interdisciplinary study of a particular geographical or national region.

4. **Colonial:** referring to a long-term period in which one society is dominated and exploited by another.

5. **Comparative politics:** an academic methodology that compares the politics, institutions, and conflicts of different countries or eras.

6. **Conjuncture:** a point of connection or coming together.

7. **Core nations:** in World Systems Theory, the developed nations at the center of the global capitalist economy.

8. **Creolization:** a process describing the emergence of Creole cultures, or cultures that combine two or more languages, in the New World. In anthropology it has come to describe general processes that involve an intentional mixture of cultural forms and identities.

9. **Cultural imperialism:** a process by which the cultural forms of a more powerful society come to dominate and perhaps replace the cultural forms of a less powerful society. The term is often associated with the prevalence of American cultural forms in the world.

10. **Culturalism:** the use of distinctive cultural identities by a group to distinguish itself from others, usually at the level of the nation-state.

11. **Cultural studies:** an interdisciplinary field of study originated by British academics in the mid-twentieth century that analyzes the idea of culture and how it is created, defined, and used. Although it draws upon anthropology, cultural studies is distinct in viewing culture not as an actual fact of human life but as an idea formed within particular times and places for reasons of

power and control.

12. **Deterritorialization:** the deconstruction of spatial boundaries associated with local, regional, or national identities or institutions.

13. **Diaspora:** a dispersed population that has a common geographical origin and a sense of shared identity associated with its history.

14. **Disjuncture:** a point of disconnect or separation.

15. **Electronic media:** technologies for the production and global distribution of media, such as satellite television and the Internet.

16. **Empirical:** refers to research or data that is based on direct experience or observation.

17. **Ethnography:** the research method used by cultural anthropologists to understand culture, usually through long-term fieldwork in a particular locale.The term also refers to the product of that research, such as a book or film.

18. **Ethnoscapes:** Appadurai's term for the distribution of people in the world, with an emphasis on immigrants, tourists, and others who are circulating globally.

19. **Financescapes:** Appadurai's term for the distribution and flow of money as it moves rapidly around the world.

20. **Fragmented:** broken into pieces. In reference to identity, this term indicates the complexity of identity, in that an individual's identity has multiple components.

21. **Frankfurt School:** a school of social theory and philosophy associated with the Institute for Social Research at Goethe University in Frankfurt, Germany, in the early to mid-twentieth century. Drawing on the work of the economist and political philosopher Karl Marx, noted for his analysis of the role of class struggle as a driver of historical events and for his critique of capitalism,

these theorists critiqued capitalism and the process of social development that it had put into place.

22. **Geographer:** someone engaged in the systematic study of the world's physical features, and the relationship of these features to the distribution of things such as population, resources, and so on.

23. **Global cultural flows:** the movement around the world of dimensions or aspects of culture, set in motion by globalization.

24. **Global ecumene:** a term introduced by anthropologist of globalization Ulf Hannerz to capture the idea that people are circulating throughout the world rather than remaining rooted in one locale. "Ecumene" is a term referring to a place inhabited by people who have made it their permanent home.

25. **Globalization:** a process by which the world is rapidly becoming more economically, politically, and culturally interconnected.

26. **Heterogenization:** a process in which cultural aspects combine and change to become more diverse.

27. **Homogenization:** a process in which cultural aspects of different societies become increasingly similar.

28. **Ideoscapes:** Appadurai's term for the shifting global landscape of political images and representations related to national or state ideologies.

29. **Imagined community:** a term coined by the nationalism scholar Benedict Anderson to describe how a group identifies as such even though its members do not all interact directly with each other (e.g. a nation.)

30. **MacArthur Fellow:** someone who receives a MacArthur Fellowship, a five-year grant awarded by the MacArthur Foundation to exceptionally creative individuals whose accomplishments speak to their ongoing future prospects.

31. **Mediascapes:** Appadurai's term for the landscape of visual narratives moving

around the world that provide substance for viewers' imagined selves and imagined worlds.

32. **Migration:** refers to the movement of individuals and groups from one place to another, either through force or voluntarily.

33. **Modernity:** a term used by scholars to refer to the late nineteenth century to the mid-twentieth century and the experience of the technological, economic, and political advances of that time.

34. **Modernization theory:** A school of theory developed in the field of sociology in the United States during the 1950s and 1960s to explain how traditional societies could develop and achieve the technological, economic, political, and other kinds of advances associated with Western societies during the mid-twentieth century.

35. **Nationalism:** an ideology expressing the strong belief that the identity or interests of an ethnic group or nation-state are of primary importance.

36. **Nation-state:** a political entity that links control over a sovereign territory (the state) with an ethnic or cultural identity (the nation).

37. **Parsimony:** refers here to research that seeks the simplest explanation for the greatest number of observations.

38. **Periphery nations:** in World Systems Theory, the developing nations on the edge of the global capitalist economy.

39. **Postcolonial:** the period after the end of colonization of one society by another.This term also refers to a scholarly perspective on the aftereffects of colonialism.

40. **Postmodernism:** a late twentieth-century trend in literary criticism, anthropology, and other academic disciplines involving a critique of the notion of universal truths. For postmodernist scholars, the meanings of representations and interpretations are not fixed but depend on perspective.

41. **Postnational:** referring to a time or situation in which the nation-state as an entity no longer exists or is much weaker than before.

42. **Primordial:** a characterization of ethnic identity based on strong attachments to a shared biological essence or kinship.

43. **Print-capitalism:** a term used by the nationalism scholar Benedict Anderson referring to the production, distribution, and consumption of newspapers, magazines, and books for an audience who all speak the same language.

44. **Rupture:** a breach or break. For Appadurai, rupture is a feature of cultures, identities, and global cultural flows today, as people and ideas break away from their original locales and come into contact with each other in new ways.

45. **"Scape":** a term coined by Appadurai to indicate the distribution and movement of things, ideas, and images around the world. It is used as a suffix in the case of words such as mediascape, technoscape, ethnoscape, etc.

46. **Social imagination:** an organized field of social practices through which individuals and communities envision and work toward new possibilities for how they want to live. For Appadurai, the social imagination is an important part of the new global order.

47. **Sociology:** the systematic study of the history, nature, and functioning of human society.

48. **Socioscapes:** a concept developed by Martin Albrow and colleagues, drawing on Appadurai, to describe the distribution and flow of social networks and relationships.

49. **Subjectivity:** an awareness, or sense of one's self and experiences, that, according to Appadurai, is shaped by culture.

50. **Technoscapes:** Appadurai's term for the distribution and movement of technologies around the world.

51. **Transnational:** moving or operating across the boundaries of nation-states.

52. **World Systems Theory:** a set of theories associated with the American sociologist Immanuel Wallerstein. It divides the world's nations into "core," "semi-periphery," and "periphery" according to their relationship to the global capitalist economy.

PEOPLE MENTIONED IN THE TEXT

1. **Martin Albrow (b. 1937)** is a British sociologist. He has published works on globalization and social change.

2. **Benedict Anderson (b. 1936)** is an American academic and professor emeritus of international studies at Cornell University. He is best known for his work on nationalism and imagined communities.

3. **Pranab Bardhan (b. 1939)** is professor of economics at the University of California at Berkeley. He has published extensively on the economics of trade, international development, and rural institutions in poor countries.

4. **Franz Boas (1858–1942)** was a German American professor of anthropology who founded the first department of anthropology in the United States at Columbia University. He is known for advancing the paradigms (conceptual models and interpretive frameworks) of historical particularism and cultural relativity that established the participant-observation method prevalent in American cultural anthropology today.

5. **Pierre Bourdieu (1930–2002)** was a French sociologist, philosopher, and anthropologist. He was known in anthropology particularly for his concept of the *habitus*, a set of cultural dispositions embodied by the individual.

6. **Carol Breckenridge (1942–2009)** was an American historian of India and the wife of Arjun Appadurai. She wrote about culture theory and colonialism, and, with Appadurai, founded *Public Culture*, a landmark journal in globalization and transnationalism studies.

7. **Mary Douglas (1921–2007)** was a British anthropologist associated with symbolic anthropology (the study of social symbols related to religion and food).

8. **Emile Durkheim (1858–1917)** was a French sociologist, an architect of modern social science, and the founder of the discipline of sociology. His theories on social solidarity and the collective conscience remain influential.

9. **E. Paul Durrenberger** is professor emeritus of anthropology at Pennsylvania State University. He has made significant contributions to the anthropology

of globalization, with a particular focus on labor.

10. **Clifford Geertz (1926–2006)** was an American professor of anthropology at the Institute for Advanced Study at Princeton University. One of the best-known American anthropologists of all time, he was associated with symbolic anthropology, and produced major works on religion, economics, and anthropological methods.

11. **Ulf Hannerz (b. 1942)** is emeritus professor of anthropology at the University of Stockholm. He is known for his contributions to the study of culture and globalization.

12. **Karl Marx (1818–83)** was a philosopher and economist of Prussian origin. He wrote enduring works on capitalism and communism and the nature of historical change.

13. **Peter Metcalf** is emeritus professor of anthropology at the University of Virginia. He has published works on comparative religion and Southeast Asia.

14. **Gijsbert Oonk** is associate professor of African and South Asian History at the Erasmus School of History, Culture, and Communication in the Netherlands. He has published works on Indian history and globalization.

15. **Isha Ray** is professor of energy and resources at the University of California at Berkeley. Her areas of expertise include water, development, and gender.

16. **Amartya Sen (b. 1933)** is an Indian economist and philosopher who is currently a professor at Harvard University. He has published widely on development issues, for both an academic and public audience, and was awarded the Nobel Memorial Prize in 1998 for his work on welfare economics.

17. **John Tomlinson** is emeritus professor of cultural sociology in the English culture and media program at Nottingham Trent University in Great Britain. He has written on globalization and culture, and has served as a consultant for national and international organizations, including UNESCO.

18. **Immanuel Wallerstein (b. 1930)** is an American sociologist. He developed World Systems Theory, a landmark approach for studying the unequal relations between nations in the global capitalist economy.

19. **Max Weber (1864–1920)** was a German philosopher who contributed greatly to social theory and helped found the discipline of sociology. He is well known for his contributions to studies of economics and religion in Western industrial nations.

WORKS CITED

1. Albrow, Martin. *The Global Age: State and Society beyond Modernity*. Stanford, CA: Stanford University Press, 1996.

2. ———. "Review: *Modernity at Large: Cultural Dimensions of Globalization* by Arjun Appadurai." *American Journal of Sociology* 103, no. 5 (March 1998): 1411–12.

3. Appadurai, Arjun. "Disjuncture and Difference in the Global Cultural Economy." *Theory, Culture, and Society* 7, no. 2 (June 1990): 295–310.

4. ———. *Fear of Small Numbers: An Essay on the Geography of Anger*. Durham, NC: Duke University Press, 2006.

5. ———. *The Future as Cultural Fact: Essays on the Global Condition* (New York: Verso, 2013).

6. ———. "Grassroots Globalization and the Research Imagination." In *Globalization*, edited by Arjun Appadurai. Durham, NC: Duke University Press, 2001.

7. ———.*Globalization*. Durham, NC: Duke University Press, 2001.

8. ———. "Illusion of Permanence: Interview with Arjun Appadurai." *Perspecta* 34 (2003): 44–52.

9. ———. *Modernity at Large: Cultural Dimensions of Globalization*. Minneapolis: University of Minnesota Press, 1996.

10. Bardhan, Pranab, and Isha Ray. "Methodological Approaches in Economics and Anthropology." *Q Squared Working Paper* 17. Centre for International Studies, University of Toronto, February 2006.

11. De Zoysa, D. A. "Review of *Modernity at Large: Cultural Dimensions of Globalization* by Arjun Appadurai." *International Migration Review* 32, no. 4 (Winter 1998): 1073–4.

12. Durrenberger, E. Paul. "Review: Anthropology and Globalization." *American Anthropologist* 103, no. 1 (June 2001): 531–5.

13. Hannerz, Ulf. *Cultural Complexity: Studies in the Social Organization of Meaning*. New York: Columbia University Press, 1992.

14. Hawley, John C. "Postscript: An Interview with Arjun Appadurai." In *The Postcolonial and the Global*, edited by Revathi Krishnaswamy and John C. Hawley. Minneapolis: University of Minnesota Press, 2007.

15. Metcalf, Peter. "Global 'Disjuncture' and the 'Sites' of Anthropology." *Cultural*

Anthropology 16, no. 2: 165–82.

16. Oonk, Gisjbert. "Review of *Modernity at Large: Cultural Dimensions of Globalization* by Arjun Appadurai." *Journal of World History* 11, no. 1 (Spring 2000): 157–9.

17. Sen, Amartya. "How Does Culture Matter?" In *Culture and Public Action*, edited by Viyarendra Rao and Michael Walton. Stanford: Stanford University Press, 2004.

18. Tomlinson, John. "Internationalism, Globalization, and Cultural Imperialism." In *Media and Cultural Regulation*, edited by Kenneth Thompson. London: Sage Publications, 1997.

原书作者简介

阿尔君·阿帕杜莱，1949 年出生于印度孟买，18 岁时来到美国。他在印度长大，成年后来到美国，经常在这两个国家之间穿梭往返。独特的人生经历使他对于人们在全球化的世界中如何看待自己和彼此有了全新的体悟，并发展出了一套充满创新性的理论。他曾先后执教于芝加哥大学和纽约大学，在美国学术界享有美誉。他的学术观点掀起了文化人类学研究的革命，并深受有志研究全球化对世界各地不同国家与社会影响的社会科学家们的欢迎。

本书作者简介

艾米·杨·埃夫拉尔拥有哈佛大学人类学博士学位，现任宾夕法尼亚葛底斯堡学院人类学副教授。

世界名著中的批判性思维

《世界思想宝库钥匙丛书》致力于深入浅出地阐释全世界著名思想家的观点，不论是谁、在何处都能了解到，从而推进批判性思维发展。

《世界思想宝库钥匙丛书》与世界顶尖大学的一流学者合作，为一系列学科中最有影响的著作推出新的分析文本，介绍其观点和影响。在这一不断扩展的系列中，每种选入的著作都代表了历经时间考验的思想典范。通过为这些著作提供必要背景、揭示原作者的学术渊源以及说明这些著作所产生的影响，本系列图书希望让读者以新视角看待这些划时代的经典之作。读者应学会思考、运用并挑战这些著作中的观点，而不是简单接受它们。

ABOUT THE AUTHOR OF THE ORIGINAL WORK

Arjun Appadurai was born in India in 1949 and moved to the United States at the age of 18. His early life in India, his adult life in the United States, and his frequent trips between the two countries, all helped to shape his innovative theories about how people see themselves and each other in a globalized world. In the course of his distinguished career in American academia, which took in posts at the University of Chicago and New York University, Appadurai's ideas have revolutionized studies in cultural anthropology and have proved popular with social scientists who want to understand how globalization affects communities around the world.

ABOUT THE AUTHOR OF THE ANALYSIS

Dr Amy Young Evrard holds a PhD in anthropology from Harvard and is currently an Associate Professor in anthropology at Gettysburg College, Pennsylvania.

ABOUT MACAT
GREAT WORKS FOR CRITICAL THINKING

Macat is focused on making the ideas of the world's great thinkers accessible and comprehensible to everybody, everywhere, in ways that promote the development of enhanced critical thinking skills.

It works with leading academics from the world's top universities to produce new analyses that focus on the ideas and the impact of the most influential works ever written across a wide variety of academic disciplines. Each of the works that sit at the heart of its growing library is an enduring example of great thinking. But by setting them in context — and looking at the influences that shaped their authors, as well as the responses they provoked — Macat encourages readers to look at these classics and game-changers with fresh eyes. Readers learn to think, engage and challenge their ideas, rather than simply accepting them.

批判性思维与《消失的现代性》

首要批判性思维技巧：创造性思维

次要批判性思维技巧：阐释

1996 年，阿尔君·阿帕杜莱出版文集《消失的现代性：全球化的文化维度》，为人类学家、地理学家、哲学家们指出了认识与理解"全球化"这当代核心话题的新路径。

全球化长期以来都被看作塑造现代世界的关键性因素——全球化是一种力量，能让商品、人口、金钱、理念与文化轻松跨越国家的边界。一方面，我们认为全球化正在重塑整个世界的形态，但是，另一方面，我们却也对其渐生疑虑——我们还不知道该如何理解与把握世界各地正在如火如荼地发生着的巨大的变化。阿帕杜莱的这本书被誉为这一领域最有影响力的著作，主要是因为它用充满创造性的方法解读了由全球化时代中深刻而快速的变化引发的问题。

创造性思维贯穿了作者写作的全过程。深谙创造性思维之道的有识之士往往会把一个问题或论点转化成为一个全新的阐释框架，阿帕杜莱就是这么做的。在《消失的现代性》一书中，阿帕杜莱从"景观"这一概念入手，对现代性进行了深入的思考和诘问。在他看来，所谓"景观"，是全球化的世界中的一套既相互独立又相互作用的流动力量，其中包括族群景观（人的流动）、媒体景观（媒体的流动）、技术景观（技术的交互作用）、金融景观（资本的流动）和意识形态景观（意识形态的流动）。通过建构起这一具有创造性的阐释框架，阿帕杜莱对全球化的真意进行了充满原创性的精彩研究与解读。

CRITICAL THINKING AND *MODERNITY AT LARGE*

• Primary critical thinking skill: CREATIVE THINKING
• Secondary critical thinking skill: INTERPRETATION

Arjun Appadurai's 1996 collection of essays *Modernity At Large: Cultural Dimensions of Globalization* helped reshape how anthropologists, geographers and philosophers saw and understood the key topic of our times: globalization.

Globalization has long been recognized as one of the crucial factors shaping the modern world—a force that allows goods, people, money, information and culture can flow across borders with relative ease. But if globalization is reshaping the world, it is also viewed with increasing suspicion—and it is still not clear how to understand and conceptualise the huge shifts that are taking place. Appadurai's work is now considered one of the most influential contributions to the field, largely because of its brilliantly creative approach to the conceptual problems posed by the deep and rapid changes that are involved.

Critical thinking lies at the heart of the author's approach to his writing. A common tactic among gifted creative thinkers is to shift a problem or argument into a novel interpretative framework, and this is exactly what Appadurai did. *Modernity at Large* interrogates modernity through Appadurai's notion of 'scapes,' a set of separate, interacting flows that, he suggests, cross the globalized world: ethnoscapes (the flow of people), mediascapes (flow of media), technoscapes (technological interactions), financescapes (capital flow), and ideoscapes (the flow of ideologies). By constructing this creative framework, it becomes possible to undertake, as Appadurai does, a brilliant and original investigation of what globalization really means.

《世界思想宝库钥匙丛书》简介

《世界思想宝库钥匙丛书》致力于为一系列在各领域产生重大影响的人文社科类经典著作提供独特的学术探讨。每一本读物都不仅仅是原经典著作的内容摘要，而是介绍并深入研究原经典著作的学术渊源、主要观点和历史影响。这一丛书的目的是提供一套学习资料，以促进读者掌握批判性思维，从而更全面、深刻地去理解重要思想。

每一本读物分为 3 个部分：学术渊源、学术思想和学术影响，每个部分下有 4 个小节。这些章节旨在从各个方面研究原经典著作及其反响。

由于体例独特，每一本读物不但易于阅读，而且另有一项优点：所有读物的编排体例相同，读者在进行某个知识层面的调查或研究时可交叉参阅多本该丛书中的相关读物，从而开启跨领域研究的路径。

为了方便阅读，每本读物最后还列出了术语表和人名表（在书中则以星号 * 标记），此外还有参考文献。

《世界思想宝库钥匙丛书》与剑桥大学合作，理清了批判性思维的要点，即如何通过 6 种技能来进行有效思考。其中 3 种技能让我们能够理解问题，另 3 种技能让我们有能力解决问题。这 6 种技能合称为"批判性思维 PACIER 模式"，它们是：

分析：了解如何建立一个观点；

评估：研究一个观点的优点和缺点；

阐释：对意义所产生的问题加以理解；

创造性思维：提出新的见解，发现新的联系；

解决问题：提出切实有效的解决办法；

理性化思维：创建有说服力的观点。

THE MACAT LIBRARY

The Macat Library is a series of unique academic explorations of seminal works in the humanities and social sciences — books and papers that have had a significant and widely recognised impact on their disciplines. It has been created to serve as much more than just a summary of what lies between the covers of a great book. It illuminates and explores the influences on, ideas of, and impact of that book. Our goal is to offer a learning resource that encourages critical thinking and fosters a better, deeper understanding of important ideas.

Each publication is divided into three Sections: Influences, Ideas, and Impact. Each Section has four Modules. These explore every important facet of the work, and the responses to it.

This Section-Module structure makes a Macat Library book easy to use, but it has another important feature. Because each Macat book is written to the same format, it is possible (and encouraged!) to cross-reference multiple Macat books along the same lines of inquiry or research. This allows the reader to open up interesting interdisciplinary pathways.

To further aid your reading, lists of glossary terms and people mentioned are included at the end of this book (these are indicated by an asterisk [*] throughout) — as well as a list of works cited.

Macat has worked with the University of Cambridge to identify the elements of critical thinking and understand the ways in which six different skills combine to enable effective thinking.

Three allow us to fully understand a problem; three more give us the tools to solve it. Together, these six skills make up the PACIER model of critical thinking. They are:

ANALYSIS — understanding how an argument is built
EVALUATION — exploring the strengths and weaknesses of an argument
INTERPRETATION — understanding issues of meaning
CREATIVE THINKING — coming up with new ideas and fresh connections
PROBLEM-SOLVING — producing strong solutions
REASONING — creating strong arguments

"《世界思想宝库钥匙丛书》提供了独一无二的跨学科学习和研究工具。它介绍那些革新了各自学科研究的经典著作，还邀请全世界一流专家和教育机构进行严谨的分析，为每位读者打开世界顶级教育的大门。"

—— 安德烈亚斯·施莱歇尔，
经济合作与发展组织教育与技能司司长

"《世界思想宝库钥匙丛书》直面大学教育的巨大挑战……他们组建了一支精干而活跃的学者队伍，来推出在研究广度上颇具新意的教学材料。"

—— 布罗尔斯教授、勋爵，剑桥大学前校长

"《世界思想宝库钥匙丛书》的愿景令人赞叹。它通过分析和阐释那些曾深刻影响人类思想以及社会、经济发展的经典文本，提供了新的学习方法。它推动批判性思维，这对于任何社会和经济体来说都是至关重要的。这就是未来的学习方法。"

—— 查尔斯·克拉克阁下，英国前教育大臣

"对于那些影响了各自领域的著作，《世界思想宝库钥匙丛书》能让人们立即了解到围绕那些著作展开的评论性言论，这让该系列图书成为在这些领域从事研究的师生们不可或缺的资源。"

—— 威廉·特朗佐教授，加利福尼亚大学圣地亚哥分校

"Macat offers an amazing first-of-its-kind tool for interdisciplinary learning and research. Its focus on works that transformed their disciplines and its rigorous approach, drawing on the world's leading experts and educational institutions, opens up a world-class education to anyone."

—— Andreas Schleicher, Director for Education and Skills, Organisation for Economic Co-operation and Development

"Macat is taking on some of the major challenges in university education... They have drawn together a strong team of active academics who are producing teaching materials that are novel in the breadth of their approach."

—— Prof Lord Broers, former Vice-Chancellor of the University of Cambridge

"The Macat vision is exceptionally exciting. It focuses upon new modes of learning which analyse and explain seminal texts which have profoundly influenced world thinking and so social and economic development. It promotes the kind of critical thinking which is essential for any society and economy. This is the learning of the future."

—— Rt Hon Charles Clarke, former UK Secretary of State for Education

"The Macat analyses provide immediate access to the critical conversation surrounding the books that have shaped their respective discipline, which will make them an invaluable resource to all of those, students and teachers, working in the field."

—— Prof William Tronzo, University of California at San Diego

The Macat Library
世界思想宝库钥匙丛书

TITLE	中文书名	类别
An Analysis of Arjun Appadurai's *Modernity at Large: Cultural Dimensions of Globalization*	解析阿尔君·阿帕杜莱《消失的现代性：全球化的文化维度》	人类学
An Analysis of Claude Lévi-Strauss's *Structural Anthropology*	解析克劳德·列维-斯特劳斯《结构人类学》	人类学
An Analysis of Marcel Mauss's *The Gift*	解析马塞尔·莫斯《礼物》	人类学
An Analysis of Jared M. Diamond's *Guns, Germs, and Steel: The Fate of Human Societies*	解析贾雷德·M.戴蒙德《枪炮、病菌与钢铁：人类社会的命运》	人类学
An Analysis of Clifford Geertz's *The Interpretation of Cultures*	解析克利福德·格尔茨《文化的解释》	人类学
An Analysis of Philippe Ariès's *Centuries of Childhood: A Social History of Family Life*	解析菲力浦·阿利埃斯《儿童的世纪：旧制度下的儿童和家庭生活》	人类学
An Analysis of W. Chan Kim & Renée Mauborgne's *Blue Ocean Strategy*	解析金伟灿/勒妮·莫博涅《蓝海战略》	商业
An Analysis of John P. Kotter's *Leading Change*	解析约翰·P.科特《领导变革》	商业
An Analysis of Michael E. Porter's *Competitive Strategy: Techniques for Analyzing Industries and Competitors*	解析迈克尔·E.波特《竞争战略：分析产业和竞争对手的技术》	商业
An Analysis of Jean Lave & Etienne Wenger's *Situated Learning: Legitimate Peripheral Participation*	解析琼·莱夫/艾蒂纳·温格《情境学习：合法的边缘性参与》	商业
An Analysis of Douglas McGregor's *The Human Side of Enterprise*	解析道格拉斯·麦格雷戈《企业的人性面》	商业
An Analysis of Milton Friedman's *Capitalism and Freedom*	解析米尔顿·弗里德曼《资本主义与自由》	商业
An Analysis of Ludwig von Mises's *The Theory of Money and Credit*	解析路德维希·冯·米塞斯《货币和信用理论》	经济学
An Analysis of Adam Smith's *The Wealth of Nations*	解析亚当·斯密《国富论》	经济学
An Analysis of Thomas Piketty's *Capital in the Twenty-First Century*	解析托马斯·皮凯蒂《21世纪资本论》	经济学
An Analysis of Nassim Nicholas Taleb's *The Black Swan: The Impact of the Highly Improbable*	解析纳西姆·尼古拉斯·塔勒布《黑天鹅：如何应对不可预知的未来》	经济学
An Analysis of Ha-Joon Chang's *Kicking Away the Ladder*	解析张夏准《富国陷阱：发达国家为何踢开梯子》	经济学
An Analysis of Thomas Robert Malthus's *An Essay on the Principle of Population*	解析托马斯·罗伯特·马尔萨斯《人口论》	经济学

An Analysis of John Maynard Keynes's *The General Theory of Employment, Interest and Money*	解析约翰·梅纳德·凯恩斯《就业、利息和货币通论》	经济学
An Analysis of Milton Friedman's *The Role of Monetary Policy*	解析米尔顿·弗里德曼《货币政策的作用》	经济学
An Analysis of Burton G. Malkiel's *A Random Walk Down Wall Street*	解析伯顿·G.马尔基尔《漫步华尔街》	经济学
An Analysis of Friedrich A. Hayek's *The Road to Serfdom*	解析弗里德里希·A.哈耶克《通往奴役之路》	经济学
An Analysis of Charles P. Kindleberger's *Manias, Panics, and Crashes: A History of Financial Crises*	解析查尔斯·P.金德尔伯格《疯狂、惊恐和崩溃：金融危机史》	经济学
An Analysis of Amartya Sen's *Development as Freedom*	解析阿马蒂亚·森《以自由看待发展》	经济学
An Analysis of Rachel Carson's *Silent Spring*	解析蕾切尔·卡森《寂静的春天》	地理学
An Analysis of Charles Darwin's *On the Origin of Species: by Means of Natural Selection, or The Preservation of Favoured Races in the Struggle for Life*	解析查尔斯·达尔文《物种起源》	地理学
An Analysis of World Commission on Environment and Development's *The Brundtland Report, Our Common Future*	解析世界环境与发展委员会《布伦特兰报告：我们共同的未来》	地理学
An Analysis of James E. Lovelock's *Gaia: A New Look at Life on Earth*	解析詹姆斯·E.拉伍洛克《盖娅：地球生命的新视野》	地理学
An Analysis of Paul Kennedy's *The Rise and Fall of the Great Powers: Economic Change and Military Conflict from 1500–2000*	解析保罗·肯尼迪《大国的兴衰：1500—2000年的经济变革与军事冲突》	历史
An Analysis of Janet L. Abu-Lughod's *Before European Hegemony: The World System A. D. 1250–1350*	解析珍妮特·L.阿布—卢格霍德《欧洲霸权之前：1250—1350年的世界体系》	历史
An Analysis of Alfred W. Crosby's *The Columbian Exchange: Biological and Cultural Consequences of 1492*	解析艾尔弗雷德·W.克罗斯比《哥伦布大交换：1492年以后的生物影响和文化冲击》	历史
An Analysis of Tony Judt's *Postwar: A History of Europe since 1945*	解析托尼·朱特《战后欧洲史》	历史
An Analysis of Richard J. Evans's *In Defence of History*	解析理查德·J.艾文斯《捍卫历史》	历史
An Analysis of Eric Hobsbawm's *The Age of Revolution: Europe 1789–1848*	解析艾瑞克·霍布斯鲍姆《革命的年代：欧洲1789—1848年》	历史

An Analysis of Roland Barthes's *Mythologies*	解析罗兰·巴特《神话学》	文学与批判理论
An Analysis of Simone de Beauvoir's *The Second Sex*	解析西蒙娜·德·波伏娃《第二性》	文学与批判理论
An Analysis of Edward W. Said's *Orientalism*	解析爱德华·W.萨义德《东方主义》	文学与批判理论
An Analysis of Virginia Woolf's *A Room of One's Own*	解析弗吉尼亚·伍尔芙《一间自己的房间》	文学与批判理论
An Analysis of Judith Butler's *Gender Trouble*	解析朱迪斯·巴特勒《性别麻烦》	文学与批判理论
An Analysis of Ferdinand de Saussure's *Course in General Linguistics*	解析费尔迪南·德·索绪尔《普通语言学教程》	文学与批判理论
An Analysis of Susan Sontag's *On Photography*	解析苏珊·桑塔格《论摄影》	文学与批判理论
An Analysis of Walter Benjamin's *The Work of Art in the Age of Mechanical Reproduction*	解析瓦尔特·本雅明《机械复制时代的艺术作品》	文学与批判理论
An Analysis of W. E. B. Du Bois's *The Souls of Black Folk*	解析W.E.B.杜波依斯《黑人的灵魂》	文学与批判理论
An Analysis of Plato's *The Republic*	解析柏拉图《理想国》	哲学
An Analysis of Plato's *Symposium*	解析柏拉图《会饮篇》	哲学
An Analysis of Aristotle's *Metaphysics*	解析亚里士多德《形而上学》	哲学
An Analysis of Aristotle's *Nicomachean Ethics*	解析亚里士多德《尼各马可伦理学》	哲学
An Analysis of Immanuel Kant's *Critique of Pure Reason*	解析伊曼努尔·康德《纯粹理性批判》	哲学
An Analysis of Ludwig Wittgenstein's *Philosophical Investigations*	解析路德维希·维特根斯坦《哲学研究》	哲学
An Analysis of G. W. F. Hegel's *Phenomenology of Spirit*	解析G.W.F.黑格尔《精神现象学》	哲学
An Analysis of Baruch Spinoza's *Ethics*	解析巴鲁赫·斯宾诺莎《伦理学》	哲学
An Analysis of Hannah Arendt's *The Human Condition*	解析汉娜·阿伦特《人的境况》	哲学
An Analysis of G. E. M. Anscombe's *Modern Moral Philosophy*	解析G.E.M.安斯康姆《现代道德哲学》	哲学
An Analysis of David Hume's *An Enquiry Concerning Human Understanding*	解析大卫·休谟《人类理解研究》	哲学

An Analysis of Søren Kierkegaard's *Fear and Trembling*	解析索伦·克尔凯郭尔《恐惧与战栗》	哲学
An Analysis of René Descartes's *Meditations on First Philosophy*	解析勒内·笛卡尔《第一哲学沉思录》	哲学
An Analysis of Friedrich Nietzsche's *On the Genealogy of Morality*	解析弗里德里希·尼采《论道德的谱系》	哲学
An Analysis of Gilbert Ryle's *The Concept of Mind*	解析吉尔伯特·赖尔《心的概念》	哲学
An Analysis of Thomas Kuhn's *The Structure of Scientific Revolutions*	解析托马斯·库恩《科学革命的结构》	哲学
An Analysis of John Stuart Mill's *Utilitarianism*	解析约翰·斯图亚特·穆勒《功利主义》	哲学
An Analysis of Aristotle's *Politics*	解析亚里士多德《政治学》	政治学
An Analysis of Niccolò Machiavelli's *The Prince*	解析尼科洛·马基雅维利《君主论》	政治学
An Analysis of Karl Marx's *Capital*	解析卡尔·马克思《资本论》	政治学
An Analysis of Benedict Anderson's *Imagined Communities*	解析本尼迪克特·安德森《想象的共同体》	政治学
An Analysis of Samuel P. Huntington's *The Clash of Civilizations and the Remaking of World Order*	解析塞缪尔·P.亨廷顿《文明的冲突与世界秩序的重建》	政治学
An Analysis of Alexis de Tocqueville's *Democracy in America*	解析阿列克西·德·托克维尔《论美国的民主》	政治学
An Analysis of John A. Hobson's *Imperialism: A Study*	解析约翰·A.霍布森《帝国主义》	政治学
An Analysis of Thomas Paine's *Common Sense*	解析托马斯·潘恩《常识》	政治学
An Analysis of John Rawls's *A Theory of Justice*	解析约翰·罗尔斯《正义论》	政治学
An Analysis of Francis Fukuyama's *The End of History and the Last Man*	解析弗朗西斯·福山《历史的终结与最后的人》	政治学
An Analysis of John Locke's *Two Treatises of Government*	解析约翰·洛克《政府论》	政治学
An Analysis of Sun Tzu's *The Art of War*	解析孙武《孙子兵法》	政治学
An Analysis of Henry Kissinger's *World Order: Reflections on the Character of Nations and the Course of History*	解析亨利·基辛格《世界秩序》	政治学
An Analysis of Jean-Jacques Rousseau's *The Social Contract*	解析让-雅克·卢梭《社会契约论》	政治学

An Analysis of Odd Arne Westad's *The Global Cold War: Third World Interventions and the Making of Our Times*	解析文安立《全球冷战：美苏对第三世界的干涉与当代世界的形成》	政治学
An Analysis of Sigmund Freud's *The Interpretation of Dreams*	解析西格蒙德·弗洛伊德《梦的解析》	心理学
An Analysis of William James' *The Principles of Psychology*	解析威廉·詹姆斯《心理学原理》	心理学
An Analysis of Philip Zimbardo's *The Lucifer Effect*	解析菲利普·津巴多《路西法效应》	心理学
An Analysis of Leon Festinger's *A Theory of Cognitive Dissonance*	解析利昂·费斯汀格《认知失调论》	心理学
An Analysis of Richard H. Thaler & Cass R. Sunstein's *Nudge: Improving Decisions about Health, Wealth, and Happiness*	解析理查德·H. 泰勒／卡斯·R. 桑斯坦《助推：如何做出有关健康、财富和幸福的更优决策》	心理学
An Analysis of Gordon Allport's *The Nature of Prejudice*	解析高尔登·奥尔波特《偏见的本质》	心理学
An Analysis of Steven Pinker's *The Better Angels of Our Nature: Why Violence Has Declined*	解析斯蒂芬·平克《人性中的善良天使：暴力为什么会减少》	心理学
An Analysis of Stanley Milgram's *Obedience to Authority*	解析斯坦利·米尔格拉姆《对权威的服从》	心理学
An Analysis of Betty Friedan's *The Feminine Mystique*	解析贝蒂·弗里丹《女性的奥秘》	心理学
An Analysis of David Riesman's *The Lonely Crowd. A Study of the Changing American Character*	解析大卫·理斯曼《孤独的人群：美国人社会性格演变之研究》	社会学
An Analysis of Franz Boas's *Race, Language and Culture*	解析弗朗兹·博厄斯《种族、语言与文化》	社会学
An Analysis of Pierre Bourdieu's *Outline of a Theory of Practice*	解析皮埃尔·布尔迪厄《实践理论大纲》	社会学
An Analysis of Max Weber's *The Protestant Ethic and the Spirit of Capitalism*	解析马克斯·韦伯《新教伦理与资本主义精神》	社会学
An Analysis of Jane Jacobs's *The Death and Life of Great American Cities*	解析简·雅各布斯《美国大城市的死与生》	社会学
An Analysis of C. Wright Mills's *The Sociological Imagination*	解析C. 赖特·米尔斯《社会学的想象力》	社会学
An Analysis of Robert E. Lucas Jr.'s *Why Doesn't Capital Flow from Rich to Poor Countries?*	解析小罗伯特·E. 卢卡斯《为何资本不从富国流向穷国？》	社会学

An Analysis of Émile Durkheim's *On Suicide*	解析埃米尔·迪尔凯姆《自杀论》	社会学
An Analysis of Eric Hoffer's *The True Believer: Thoughts on the Nature of Mass Movements*	解析埃里克·霍弗《狂热分子：群众运动圣经》	社会学
An Analysis of Jared M. Diamond's *Collapse: How Societies Choose to Fail or Survive*	解析贾雷德·M.戴蒙德《大崩溃：社会如何选择兴亡》	社会学
An Analysis of Michel Foucault's *The History of Sexuality Vol. 1: The Will to Knowledge*	解析米歇尔·福柯《性史（第一卷）：求知意志》	社会学
An Analysis of Michel Foucault's *Discipline and Punish*	解析米歇尔·福柯《规训与惩罚》	社会学
An Analysis of Richard Dawkins's *The Selfish Gene*	解析理查德·道金斯《自私的基因》	社会学
An Analysis of Antonio Gramsci's *Prison Notebooks*	解析安东尼奥·葛兰西《狱中札记》	社会学
An Analysis of Augustine's *Confessions*	解析奥古斯丁《忏悔录》	神学
An Analysis of C. S. Lewis's *The Abolition of Man*	解析 C. S. 路易斯《人之废》	神学

图书在版编目（CIP）数据

解析阿尔君·阿帕杜莱《消失的现代性：全球化的文化维度》/艾米·杨·埃夫拉尔（Amy Young Evrard）著；李磊译. —上海：上海外语教育出版社，2019
（世界思想宝库钥匙丛书）
ISBN 978−7−5446−6012−9

Ⅰ.①解… Ⅱ.①艾… ②李… Ⅲ.①全球化−研究 Ⅳ.①C913

中国版本图书馆CIP数据核字（2019）第215972号

This Chinese-English bilingual edition of *An Analysis of Arjun Appadurai's* Modernity at Large is published by arrangement with MACAT International Limited.
Licensed for sale throughout the world.

本书汉英双语版由Macat国际有限公司授权上海外语教育出版社有限公司出版。供在全世界范围内发行、销售。

图字：09−2018−549

出版发行：上海外语教育出版社
（上海外国语大学内） 邮编：200083
电　　话：021−65425300（总机）
电子邮箱：bookinfo@sflep.com.cn
网　　址：http://www.sflep.com
责任编辑：张　宏

印　　刷：上海信老印刷厂
开　　本：890×1240　1/32　印张 5.25　字数 107千字
版　　次：2020 年 8 月第 1 版　　2020 年 8 月第 1 次印刷
印　　数：2 100 册

书　　号：ISBN 978-7-5446-6012-9
定　　价：30.00 元

本版图书如有印装质量问题，可向本社调换
质量服务热线：4008-213-263　电子邮箱：editorial@sflep.com